Customer Service: The Reason Some HBCUs are Destined to Fail

Dr. Tracy Andrus

North-Star Publishing
104 Johnson Street
Marshall, Texas 75670

Fall 2015

Acknowledgement

A special thank you to the authors of this book who submitted chapters in this book. This work has taken almost two years to come to fruition but it is now here. To Drs. Dan, Piper, Scott, Guerrero, Burnett-Andrus, Divine and Mr. Venders and Ms. Alaniz, I am very thankful to you all for your contributions to this book. I pray that each of you will be successful in your future publication endeavors!

Dr. Tracy Andrus

Dedication

This book is dedicated to the memory of my Mother the late Ms. Alice V. Andrus (8-25-1926) – (1-1-2015) and my two sisters Ms. Josephine Ledet (7-7-1947) – (11-27-2014) and Ms. Elouise Beverly (12-03-1940) - (1-30-2015) whom I lost all within the last year. Rest in Peace!

Index

Foreword

Foreword

Customer Service The Reason Some HBCUs Are Destined to Fail

By

Daniel E. Georges-Abeyie, Ph.D.

Professor of Administration of Justice

Texas Southern University

Introduction

It is, indeed, a pleasure, to write the foreword to **Customer Service and Why Some HBCUs Are Destined to Fail** edited by Dr. Tracy Andrus, Director, Associate Professor, Lee P. Brown Criminal Justice Institute, Wiley College, in that this author has served as the former Associate Dean of the College of Juvenile Justice and Psychology, and the Interim Chair, Department of Psychology, the Prairie View A & M University, while also holding the rank of tenured Full Professor, the Department of Juvenile Justice. It was a privilege to serve as the first Associate Dean of the College of Juvenile Justice and Psychology, PVAMU and as one of the first Full Professors at the educational institution, which graduated the first Ph.D. in Juvenile Justice, in the USA and the first Ph.D. in Adolescent Clinical Psychology, at an HBCU, in any nation-state, respectively, with Dr. Andrus the first Ph.D. in Juvenile Justice. **This author for more than forty years has been involved with the assessment and delivery of educational services at numerous Historic Black Colleges and Universities [HBCUs] located in USA and the British Virgin Islands [BVI]**, ranging from Texas Southern University, Houston Texas, where this author helped develop and coordinate the first Ph.D. in Administration of Justice in an HBCU and while serving as the first Chair for the Department of Administration of Justice, and continues to serve as a senior Full Professor. It has also been this author's privilege to serve his beloved H. L. Stoutt Community College, an HBCU, located on Tortola, British Virgin Islands [BVI], his homeland, with H. L. Stoutt, a fully accredited academic institution and community service friendly institution, directed by the very able President, Dr. Karl Dawson, this author's cousin, who has coordinated interface with the University of the West Indies, located on the H. L. Stoutt campus and with elite USA institutions, including this author's Ph.D. alma mater, Syracuse University. Perhaps most importantly, with regard to credibility in writing a foreword to this very important book, this author has successfully served through the ranks of academe as an academician and administrator [at least thirteen times], since 1971 at such prestigious **majority race** colleges and universities as the Johns Hopkins University, Amherst College, the Pennsylvania State University, SUNY-Albany, two campuses of the California State University System, Arizona State University, Southern Illinois University at Carbondale, the Florida State University, and a campus of the City University of New York and two **HBCUs,** Prairie View A&M University and Texas Southern University.

The "Why" in the Title of the Foreword

The "Why" in the title of the foreword results in two meanings, one historic and the other current. **The historic meaning of "Why"** refers to the reason for the existence of HBCUs, with which many of the readers of this edited volume are familiar; i.e., the **reality, if not intent,** of Plessy v. Ferguson, separate but unequal accommodations, including state, federal, and private educational accommodations, which directly, or indirectly, resulted in the receipt of various forms of direct and indirect federal support, including financial support by HBCUs. Put simply, blacks were excluded from enrollment [or severely limited with regard to enrollment] at many state, federal, and private universities and colleges, which received federal funding, in some form, or were gifted with the placement of various federal research, policy, and service

6

institutions, resulting in the need for higher educational institutions that enrolled black students. **The current "Why"** in the title of this foreword asks and addresses "why" HBCUs continue to exist, are they necessary, or even desirable in 2015, when many, if not most, or all, of these institutions are grossly underfunded, and the vast majority of these HBCUs are ranked as forth tier institutions, with regard to **educational quality, or perceived educational quality,** by those agencies and agents [such as high school guidance counselors and career counselors, the **US News and World Report**, et cetera], while several HBCUs are not ranked at all, for various reason, with regard to educational quality. Perhaps, even more disturbing is 1) educational outcomes, such as percent of students who graduate in six years; percent of students full-time employed, six months after graduation, much less employed full-time in an occupation related to their major; pathetically low HBCU alumni scores on ETS examinations in respective academic majors/disciplines, much less HBCU alumni scores with regard to percentile in the discipline compared with alumni graduating from majority race colleges and universities; equally disturbing is 2) the retention of regional accreditation and state and federal funding formulae have resulted **in inordinate pressure to improve, that is, elevate, at all costs,** six year graduation rates for undergraduates and the modal number of annual undergraduate alumni, professional school/program alumni, and graduate school alumni, with the concomitant **pressure to inflate grades**, that is, pass virtually every student who exhibits the most infinitesimal effort at class attendance. The aforementioned, practices, now administration directed policies mandated from chairs, deans, vice presidents, provosts, and presidents have resulted in **a culture, not subculture, of expectation, of entitlement,** with university administrations compiling lists that note instructors who give failing grades, not just an inordinate number of failing grades; i.e., grades below a "D" in undergraduate courses and/or below "B" in graduate courses or professional school courses. The aforementioned practices have doomed HBCU graduates to employment failure and lack of competitiveness with alumni of majority race colleges and universities, which have their own funding and grading pressures. The aforementioned negative outcomes have been bitterly expressed to this author at every academic discipline gathering attended, such as the ASC, ACJS, APA, BCJ [Blacks in Criminal Justice], the AAG, et cetera. Similar statements of best educational outcome concerns/best teaching/learning practices have been expressed to this author at every HBCU visited over the last forty, or so, years, by highly qualified HBCU faculty and professional staff. This author's students, polled at TSU, every year, for the last eight years, when asked "'Why they opted to attend TSU?", stated 1) to get a degree [ninety-five percent], 2) my parents or a relative attended TSU [three percent], other reason [such as college fair presentation, radio or TV advertisement, et cetera, one percent], the superior/outstanding educational practices and educational and outcomes/reputation for academic excellence provided by TSU; usually expressed as a variant of student centered education, one percent], and **acquisition of knowledge [zero percent]**. This author suspects, based upon conversations with students, indeed a universe almost as limited and lacking in polling rigor, as students enrolled in some of the courses taught by this author, if "availability of financial aid" was an option, it would be the first, or second, most frequently selected answer to the aforementioned query. The key point being, educational quality, acquisition of knowledge, and reputation for academic excellence, individually, or collectively, are not reasons, much less primary reasons, for attending TSU, or any HBCU I have visited, with the exception of Howard University, Hampton Institute, and the Consortium of small private HBCUs in Atlanta, and H. L. Stoutt College, the British Virgin Islands, with dating potential and the potential for the selection of an African American spouse among the most common reasons voiced to this author for

8

attending a HBCU in Atlanta; a reason not to be scoffed at, in that mate selection has always been a significant priority for attending an Ivy League College/University or other elite gentile dominant institution, if WASP, or a "Wannabe" WASP, or the so-called Jewish Ivy League; e.g., Brandeis University, NYU, Syracuse University, the Pennsylvania State University, Yeshiva University, Boston University, and Columbia University and the University of Pennsylvania, two Ivy League Universities with disproportionate Jewish enrollment and very active Hillel involvement.

The Ranking of HBCUs

US News and World Report notes that "Only about 40 percent of black, Latino, and American Indian students [nationwide not just at HBCUs] receive bachelor's degree within six years" (US News, 2015. Retrieved from http://www.usnews.com/education/slideshows/hbcus-with-high-graduation-rates), with several HBCUs, such as Spelman College at 78 percent and Howard University at 70 percent exceeding the 40 percent national graduation rate for black and Latino students, which documents, in part, that educational failure, as measured by the six year graduation rate, varies by HBCUs; with exceeding the 40 percent six year graduations rate the anomaly, not the norm for HBCUs. There are significant reasons for the low six year graduation at HBCUs, including the lack of stringent entry requirements, relative to comparable majority race institutions, even amongst the 25 highest ranked HBCUs, resulting in the high percentage of students accepted for admission [a low of 21 percent at Fisk University to a high of 69 percent at Bennett College], with low to exceptionally low ACT and SAT scores, with ACT and SAT scores a significant predictor of likely success at college/university. Very few HBCU ACT and SAT admission averages meet, much less exceed, SAT and ACT thresholds for likely success at college/university. An HBCU, such as TSU, until recently practiced open admission, while currently utilizing innovative admissions practices, such as summer admission with intensified tutorial and academic advising for students with minimal ACT scores, SAT scores, and low GPA. However, few, if any HBCUs **require student attendance at tutorials or remedial classes** throughout the student's residency, should the student's GPA fall below a "C" average, although fully aware that the student will not likely voluntarily enroll in such courses. Why is mandatory enrollment necessary? The answer is, such is required for best leaning outcomes and to overcome what may be human nature. Many, if not most individuals likely view such enrollment as a self-declaration of failure, or minimally as a declaration of need, and therefore fear the less than rational insensitive reactions of peers. This, author, can vividly remember being teased by childhood peers [friends and acquaintances] in the Ft. Apache/Mott Haven/Melrose neighborhoods [Police Districts] of the predominantly Caribbean South Bronx, NYC, for parentally enforced enrollment in remedial English, ESL, diction, syntax, grammar, and mathematics courses. This author's mother was a Gullah-Geechee mother, with a six grade education [the most intelligent and most highly self-educated person this author has been privileged to know] and a Tortolan, BVI father, with a partial high school education, who spoke BVI pigeon English, Spanish, and Spanglish. Thus, ALL of this author's relatives were Gullah-Geechee, or from the Dominican Republic, Trinidad, Barbados, Puerto Rico, the Puerto Rican/Spanish Virgin Islands, the USVI, and the BVI; ALL significant others were Gullah-Geechee, Caribbean, or Mainland African. Fortunately, this author had parents that were cognizant that Standard English was not within this author's social-cultural milieu. Thus, the teasing was taken in stride, absorbed painlessly, by this author, in that **ALL significant others were family**; that is, family by blood, or **family by declaration and identity**.

HBCU Rankings 2015

The following is the **HBCU Rankings 2015: The Top 25 List from US News,** which includes 80 colleges/universities, with direct author involvement with nine of the top 25 HBCUs in the **Top 25 [HBCU] List from US News**, via site reviews, professional staff and faculty workshops, et cetera, as well as numerous various comprehensive involvement with other HBCUs in **The Top 80 [HBCU] List from US News.** "To qualify for the U.S. News HBCU rankings 2015, an HBCU must be an undergraduate baccalaureate-granting institution that primarily gives admission to first-year, first-time students and must be a school that is a part of Best Colleges rankings 2015. Moreover, a school must be currently classified by the U.S Department of Education as an HBCU.

"In total, 80 HBCUs qualified to be included on the list; out of which, 69 were ranked and 11 were unranked. These HBCUs were compared only with each other on the criteria of faculty resources, faculty salary, retention, student selectively, alumni giving, and financial resources." (US News, 2015. Retrieved http://hbculifestyle.com/hbcu-rankings-2015-top-25).

HBCU Rankings 2015

	College or University	Acceptance Rate
1	Spelman College	41%
2	Howard University	57%
3	Morehouse College	67%

4	Hampton University	36%
5	Tuskegee University	41%
6	Xavier University of Louisiana	54%
7	Fisk University	21%
8	Florida A&M University	45%
9	Claflin University	61%
10	North Carolina A&T State University	57%
11	North Carolina Central University	39%
12	Tougaloo College	34%
13	Delaware State University	45%
13	Dillard University	35%
15	Morgan State University	56
15	Winston-Salem State University	56
17	Johnson C. Smith University	37
18	Clark Atlanta University	57
19	Jackson State University	65
20	Elizabeth City State University	52
21	Lincoln University	61
21	Tennessee State University	54
23	Alabama A&M University	54
23	University of Maryland Eastern Shore	55

The Historic Why, in Why HBCUs: The More "things" Change the more "things" Remain the Same

Ironically, the **historic Why**, in **Why HBCUs** have changed, remained the same; the provision of educational opportunities for students, especially black students, with limited financial resources, limited academic admission options, limited best practices educational backgrounds, and limited best educational practices outcomes, as measured via standardized test scores, GPA, and dominant academic role-sets. Many denizens, or lifelong residents, in the world of HBCUs when confronted by demands to document best practices educational strategies and outcomes, are affronted, or at least express real or faux irritation, or outright outrage. When this author questions HBCU students about their educational practices, their learning practices/role-sets, this author uniformly observes the following, role-sets that unfortunately doom many HBCU students to current and future academic and professional failure, role-sets that transmute best practices in customer service [the provision of and enhancement of educational standards, achievement, and role-sets] to faux success and alienated faculty and professional staff:

- freshmen from high schools, which attempted to maintain order and discipline at least, if not more so, than a best practices learning environments, including best practices learning outcomes
- students from high schools with substandard educational facilities

- students from high schools with a disproportionate number of junior faculty, or faculty assigned as a result of a disciplinary action by administrators
- students who use the financial assistance offered by the HBCU as a primary or secondary source of income, with no intent by the student to earn an academic degree
- students with little, if any, realistic concept of what is meant "to study"
- students who interpret "to study" as meaning to scan or to superficially read an assignment and thereby, not ask, the significance of the reading, much less, what could be inferred from the reading
- students who neither purchase, nor have personal access to required readings and other required/assigned materials
- students who expect the provision of PowerPoint slides and other so-called study aids/assists, frequently provided by the publisher, or the professor of record for the course, which the student can, and does, substitute for instructor provided assignments
- students that expect the provision of extra credit assignments, which have peripheral, if any, centrality to the semester course curriculum, or syllabus, at the termination of the course, or upon failing, or near the conclusion of the course, when failure is a certainty or a near/likely certainty
- student expectation of a substantial curve of the final grade, so that blatant lack of achievement is transmuted into achievement, by virtual of a passing grade or inflated grade
- oppositional defiant students that resent an orderly, respectful classroom setting, in which unpopular opinions are expressed or the Socratic Method utilized

- students that expect slum ghetto role-sets and pedestrian role-sets to be placated in the classroom setting, such as late entrance and early exit from the classroom; cross conversations/ more than one person speaking at a time; the conversion of the active classroom environs into a daycare center; and outright rude unsightly behavior, including putting one's head on the table; sleeping in class; eating in classroom during the lecture; utilization of various electronic devices, such as smart telephones IPads, et cetera, for purposes other than note taking
- students that confuse the request for them to explain their opinion non-emotively and to support said opinion with facts, not other opinions, no matter how common that opinion, as an imposition or an academic interrogation
- student, staff, and faculty gossip mills, although common at all colleges and universities are especially vibrant at HBCUs

The Historic Why in Why HBCUs and Why Some HBCUs Are Destined to Fail

The **historic Why** in **Why HBCUs and Why Some HBCUs Are Destined to Fail** are firmly immersed in a structural-functional dilemma. Structural-Functional theory includes the tenet, the structure, including practices, frequently persist after their initial purpose/function. Thus, what was instrumental can, and frequently does, become dysfunctional. The initial manifestation of HBCUs for the provision of higher education for blacks during grand apartheid, during the Jim Crow Era, is no longer necessary, with regard to official admission exclusion. The provision of higher education institutions and associated services, however, rudimentary, were necessary during the Jim Crow Era. Nonetheless, a black, Latino , poor white, Asian, and Native American underclass persists in the Capitalist USA, where children of the underclass lack

15

the best practices role-sets [skills] necessary for educational achievement and employment success, in constant competitive environments. The **Why in Why HBCUs and in Why Some HBCUs Are Destined to Fail** are now clarion calls for the provision of relatively low cost high quality higher education, which results in best practices role-sets, including outcomes at HBCUs and the inculcation of best practices learning role-sets in students currently enrolled at HBCU, which result in degrees that are a statement of academic substance/acumen, with resultant high measurable educational outcomes, such as high ETS scores, if not sky high six year graduation rates [meaning some students don't learn and subsequently fail], and substantial employment after graduation for not just six months, but for multiple years.

The Provision of Customer Service: High Educational Outcomes and Limited HBCU
Failure

The answer to how to achieve **High Educational Outcomes and Limited HBCU Failure** may not be as difficult as might be anticipated, by many. **The answer is, limited educational objectives in an academic race-and-ethnic-based universe**; i.e., the unpopular, but realistic call for the return to the **original raison d'être for HBCUs**, with very, very few exceptions, i.e., **first class undergraduate education**. Simply put HBCU institutions are severely limited with regard to financial resources, such as endowment; financial rating for loans; capital funds; first rate, much less cutting edge classroom, offices, and research facilities; competitive professional staff and faculty salaries; competitive clerical and secretarial staff salaries, and are likely to become more limited with regard to financial resources, as more blacks attend majority race institutions, and transfer their loyalty to majority race colleges and universities, which translates into financial support for majority race institutions, rather HBCUs. HBCUs cannot be, or become, everything for every one! A veneer is a veneer, no matter how professionally duplicated. A veneer means an imitation! HBCUs must do what they can do best with limited resources, **teach**, provide community service, and conduct limited community-based research, which may have local impact, even profound local impact, but similar to a supreme court case, act as precedent, a profound precedent, not an educational veneer!

Specific best learning practices by HBCUs, that is, role-sets, with likely measurable best practices outcomes include, but are not be limited to the following:

- Offer a comprehensive liberal arts curriculum enhanced by an **Afrocentric Curriculum**, which may result in an **Afrocentric Research Center/Policy Center** with focused research and presentation

- Offer **African Diaspora and African Mainland curricula** with a concomitant Research Center/Policy Center, if federal funds, or state funds, are available, or likely; e.g., Black Studies; African and African Diaspora Studies; Afro Caribbean Studies; Afro Latino-Afro Francophone, and Afro Lusophone Studies, **not African American Studies**, after all, only six percent, or so, of African slaves were brought to the Northern Hemisphere, which limits potential funds from nation-states with sizeable African Diasporas populations. Frankly, how much financial/economic interest do government officials and entrepreneurs in capitalist North America have with regard to African Americans and why should so-called development nation-states take a financial interest in African America? Like it, or not, Leon Trotsky's Law of Uneven and Combined Development, a tenet of the Theory of the Permanent Revolution is correct, oppressed people are most aware of their own oppression, self-identify and act as unique self-identifying entities. Simply put, don't expect altruism.

17

- Seek to become the undergraduate honors college---magnet college---for one's state educational system, seek to become a college similar to SUNY--Geneseo or the New College of Florida, in that state capital funds are more likely than state supplied research funds and capital funds have a longer lasting impact and broader impact, on a campus, than research funds; such a college/university. A magnet university or college, in the form of an honors institution, will likely have wider appeal/more comprehensive appeal across race, ethnicity, sex, gender, or another identity criterion/delineator, such as an honors programs at college, or university, identified with a specific racial or ethnic group. .

- Limit, or eliminate, expensive graduate school and professional school curricula, such curricula are educational pyrite/fool's gold. Although educational pyrite/fool's gold results in higher formula funding than most traditional undergraduate curricula, with the exception of 100 level course/basic entry level courses [which filter out first year students] they are relatively expensive to staff and to provide with first rate/cutting edge material resources, such as first rate or cutting edge facilities at the graduate level, especially in the so-called natural/biological/hard sciences, engineering, and policy studies/area studies academic realms, which frequently require study aboard and expensive guest lecturers.

- First rate pedagogy requires **first rate teachers** and **limited course preparation** on the undergraduate level, much less at the graduate level, or undergraduate-graduate. Five-five, or even three-four teaching loads, much less heavier mandated course loads, or volunteered teaching loads [extra/additional teaching assignments], because of non-existent merit raises and non-existent cost of living faculty raises, especially when professional staff and administrators garner raises, including cost of living and merit raises, demoralizes faculty, while "forcing" faculty to self-enroll for more courses with their current employer or moonlight elsewhere. Excessive teaching loads, for whatever reason, means superficial pedagogy and overreliance on PowerPoint slides and other instructor assists provided by publishers.

- Drop, abandoned, the tripartite academic delusion of excellence in teaching, service, and scholarship, and stress excellence in teaching and service; too many HBCUs have lowered the scholarship threshold to the point of absurdity, due to the unstated realization the excellence in all three of the aforementioned, is unrealistic, delusional, or at best illusionary. Simply put, stop the farce! Most HBCU faculty cannot and do not annually publish a high quality research paper, or analysis treatises; a "scholarship" threshold, which is in itself, mundane, for a research institution, and impossible for a teaching centered college or university. Most academicians, regard less of employer, know that most academicians do not produce three such publications, much less secure grants prior to tenure; typically six year academic endeavor. The demand that HBCU faculty regularly apply for, that is, annually apply for, research grants with near zero likelihood of success, in order to meet delusional or illusionary research standard of excellence, is absurd. Zero outcomes should never be viewed as anything other than failure! Pedagogic innovation, measurable pedagogic outcomes are more likely than success with regard to securing research grants, in a learning environment populated by **high**

demand students, that is, students with very limited best educational practices learning skills, but a very elevated/highly developed sense of entitlement to a college degree, university degree, or course grade, regardless of exhibited learning outcomes. Does it not make more sense to reward successful pedagogic innovation, or tried-and-true tutorial education and remedial education, when many of our students have trouble reading, much less understanding polysyllabic sentences, including PowerPoint slides!

- Offer a unique undergraduate curricula, especially if an institution in a state system, for example GIS and Spatial/International Area Studies, rather than Geography; forensic science; administration of justice or juvenile justice curricula, rather than a generalist criminal justice curriculum, if such common educational fare are offered at neighboring, local, regional, or state institutions.

- Seek membership in a state system, rather than maintain underfunded isolation and the certainty of student enrollment atrophy and likely institutional death/non-existence; note the positive capital fund outcomes and program outcomes experienced by Prairie View A&M University, rather than the "ghost student enrollment" strategies and the desperate enrollment of previously suspended students, or dismissed students, and faux census day data, familiar to everyone familiar with state supported HBCUs, which means familiarity with precipitous student attendance decline, immediately after the student census date.

- Seek joint pedagogic initiatives with majority race institutions, perhaps as **internal study abroad** options for students at the **cooperative institutions, or institutional consortiums,** similar to the prestigious five college consortium in

Central New York, which includes Syracuse University, Cornell University, Colgate University, the University of Rochester, and Ithaca College.

- Abandon HBCU nepotism, which results in the hire; tenure; and promotion of family members, church members, members of other HBCUs, after shallow rationalizations, known to most, if not all, HBCU faculty and staff, not just professional staff, as a farce, a wired hire; the cessation in the hire of "Brother" and "Sister" members of African American fraternal orders [including sororities], after frequently ignoring faculty search committee recommendations, with regard to not only faculty hires, but the hire of professional staff and administrators.

- Immediately address the ethnic and racial schisms, with regard to administration, faculty, staff, and students, known, but ignored, on most HBCU campuses, which take pride in diversity, but make limited, if any, systematic efforts toward cultural pluralism and enhanced interaction between, and amongst, ethnic and racial identity groups, on campus.

- Implement and practice standard courtesy role-sets, including the non-closure of secretarial and clerical services between 12 Noon and 1:00 P.M., an absurd and bizarre practice common on many HBCU campuses, after all most of the USA is in a time zone other than the specific HBCU, while many persons in the HBCU time zone have a lunch break at the very time in which HBCUs close down clerical and secretarial services for lunch; i.e., simply stagger said breaks if more than one secretary or clerk is on staff, or vary the break period during the week, if the staff consists of one person.

- Implement and practice **standard Eurocentric courtesy role-sets**, which include faux caring, open welcoming body language, welcoming facial expressions, and polite utterance/clichés, such as "Hello", "Good morning" [or the like], "Can I help you?", et cetera, in that many courtesy role-sets on HBCU campuses are oppositional, or apparently oppositional, perhaps expressions of common current, working class and middle class African American secondary interaction social-cultural etiquette, which frequently, according to this author's observation and the expressed observation of this author's students, appears gruff, impersonal, impatient, uncaring, coldly indifference, and the expression of annoyance.

Conclusion

Grand apartheid, Jim Crow, helped create the HBCU; petit apartheid [customary practices for varied reasons] ironically, helped sustain it and continues to help sustain it, while too frequently assuring its demise. **Inferior customer service dooms HBCUs, in general**, if customer service can be measured by best practice outcomes of graduation rates; sustained alumni employment; state of the art facilities; reasonably paid faculty and staff; HBCU student scores on ETS exams and various licensure exams, when compared with students enrolled at, or previously enrolled at, majority race colleges and universities; reasonable teaching loads; meaningful community service and community-based research agenda; state of the art curriculums, which meet current as well as likely societal demands; endowments; and financial ratings [sometimes impacted by endowment's as collateral] that enable borrowing and funding of various projects at a reasonable interest rate…

The key to HBCU survival is to do what it can do well, excel at **teaching** and not do more with less, in that **less is almost always less**. Constant increasing curricula at the graduate school and professional school levels, and now distant learning degree programs, with limited resources, to the point that many HBCU programs lack secretarial staffs and clerical staffs, or have skeletal staffs, at the expense of undergraduate education is illogical. The aforementioned illogic is manifested in HBCU rankings, in general, and specific program rankings, in particular. Few HBCU programs/rankings are second tier, or third tier, much less first tier, which makes absolutely no sense to this author. HBCUs offered high quality educational opportunities for a disenfranchised population; they can continue to do so, while a select few HBCUs can become pedagogic magnets institutions within state systems, or within the realm of private for-profit education. Frankly, there is no reason HBCUs cannot become the SUNY-Geneseo, the New College of Florida, Elon University, UNC Asheville, Davidson College, High Point University, Salem College, Guilford College, Meredith College, or perhaps even the Appalachian State University [for those that believe large is better, if not best] of their state. Great aspirations are fine, but delusion---a false fixed belief---is a sign of madness and a waste of resources. Professor Andrus is correct, **Some HBCUs Are Destined to Fail,** if the analyses offered in this very important book are correct; this author believes the analyses to be correct. Nonetheless, not all is lost.

Chapter One

Historical Emergence of HBCUs

Dr. T. Andrus

There are 104 historically black colleges and universities (HBCU) in the United States today according to the United States Department of Education. While HBCUs represent just three percent of the nation's institutions of higher learning, they graduate nearly 20% of African Americans who earn undergraduate degrees. Congress officially defined HBCUs as institutions whose principal mission was and is the education of black Americans that are accredited and was established before 1964. Historical black colleges and universities emerged in the early 1800's with the earliest recorded HBCU being Cheyney University in Pennsylvania in 1837. Cheyney was originally established to offer only elementary and high school level instruction. It was followed by two more black institutions Lincoln University in Pennsylvania (1854), and Wilberforce University, in Ohio in (1856). Prior to 1837 very few African Americans attended institutions of higher education. Prior to the Civil War (1861-1865) very few African Americans attended college period because the vast majority of African Americans were enslaved. It was during reconstruction (1865-1877) after the civil war that opportunities for blacks to attend college began to widen.

The years between the Civil War and World War I (1914-1918) were the years that saw tremendous growth in establishing HBCUS. With the advent of public taxes supporting colleges and the historical passage of the Morrill Act of 1862 HBCU emergence began to be front and center. African Americans began to enroll in colleges and universities in record numbers. From reconstruction through World War II (1939-1945) most African Americans were enrolled in private colleges that were established by Northern religious mission associations. A very few African religious philanthropy associations also established a significant number of HBCUs.

Because of the previous lack or nonexistence of public education in the south, African Americans entering colleges were taught prepatory remedial material for years until they were ready to receive college level courses. During this era it is understandable that these newly freed slaves were not ready to master the college level materials because they were never exposed to reading and writing but it is unacceptable today in my opinion to have so many African Americans enter college unable to be placed in mainstream English and Math courses. Approximately 50% of African Americans College students are place in remedial English courses and approximately 75% are placed in remedial math courses. While it was understandable for those who were recently released from slavery to have staggering numbers of students in remedial courses it is unacceptable to have these percentages in 2015 after students have earned their high school diplomas.

Blacks during the early 1900s were trained for literacy and for professions in the north and the south. With the end of reconstruction and the return of white rule in the south the opportunities for professional jobs diminished and proponents of manual/industrial training emerged encouraging most African Americans to concentrate on getting a manual education. One of the great proponents of this era was Booker T. Washington of the Tuskegee Institute. Washington believed that African Americans should concentrate on the art of manual labor to suit them for the jobs that were available. In opposition to Washington, the Harvard trained W.E.B. Dubois accused Booker T. Washington of appeasing the white southerners and downplaying education for the African Americans in the south. Because of Dubois' militancy and outcries against Washington's theory on education protests broke out in certain parts of the

United States and students boycotted and protests against white administrations at Fisk, Hampton and Howard. As a result of these protests Mordacai Johnson was named the first Black President of Howard University in 1926.

In 1862 one year before the signing of the Emancipation Proclamation Senator Justin Morrill spearheaded a campaign to improve education in the United States. Morrill's act aimed to train students in farming, science, and education. While many institutions received land-grants and funding during this time very few were inviting to blacks, particularly in the south. Only Alcorn State University in Mississippi was created exclusively for blacks. It was nearly 28 years later before this problem would be rectified. In 1890 Senator Morrill rectified this problem by specifying that states using federal land grant funds must either make their schools open to both blacks and white or allocate money to build black colleges and universities which were to serve as alternatives to white schools. As a result of this ruling sixteen exclusive black institutions were formed and received land-grant funds.

Prior to the Morrill Act many private universities, elementary and high school were established by the American Missionary Association (AMA) and he Freedmen's Bureau. In addition to this many African American churches ran their own elementary and secondary schools for blacks which prepared them for vocations and advanced studies. The AMA, Freedmen's Bureau and black churches became the catalyst for black education and served to provide education that lasted for generations to come. Historically black colleges and universities gained credibility in 1928 when the Southern Association of Colleges and Schools began formally surveying and accrediting them in 1928.

During the periods of the Great Depression and World War II many HBCUs faced new challenges which included in part funding for their schools. It was during this era that the private

HBCUs suffered the greatest. Because of their dismal funding administrators were distracted from improving education. This period of decreased funding led Dr. Frederick Patterson, President of Tuskegee Institute to publish an open letter to the presidents of private HBCUs urging them to ban together to pool their resources and fundraising strategies. As a result of his request the United Negro fund was established and began raising millions of dollars for private HBCUs. Today this program is still effective and supports the education of thousands of deserving African American students.

Ten years later black students and HBCUs became beneficiaries of the U.S. Supreme Court's decision in the case of Brown Versus Board of Education which stated that separate but equal was anything but separate and equal. As a result of that ruling HBCUs became better funded and this ruling also paved the way for black students to begin entering majority white schools. Later the Civil Rights Act of 1964 gave the federal government greater power to enforce desegregation.

In 1965, the federal government provided aid to HBCUs through the Higher Education Act. Later the courts in the case of Adams vs. Richardson found ten states in violation of the Civil Rights Act for supporting desegregated schools. Those ten states were ordered to work at integrating their institutions. In recent years the Carter, Regan, Bush, Clinton, Bush 2 and Obama Administrations have all worked to strengthen and expand the capacity of historical black colleges and universities. Each administration has orchestrated executive orders to reverse the effects of previous discriminatory treatment of black colleges.

Another pivotal ruling came in 1992 in the case of United States vs. Fordice in which the Supreme Court ruled that Mississippi must do away with the remnants of a dual segregated system of education. The courts as well as the black citizens of Mississippi realized that HBCUs provided a very unique education for African Americans. HBCUs graduated African-Americans more frequently than predominantly white universities and gave the students more academic support. Therefore the courts realized that HBCUs in that respect must continue to be protected because not only were they a part of American history, but they will also play an important part in America's future.

Accomplishments of HBCUs

- More than 80% of all black Americans who received degrees in medicine and dentistry were trained at the two traditionally black institutions of medicine and dentistry – Howard University and Meharry Medical College. Today these institutions still account for 19.7 percent of degrees awarded in medicine and dentistry to black students.
- HBCUs have provided undergraduate training for 75% of all black persons holding doctorate degree; 75% of all black officers in the armed forces; and 80% of all black judges.
- HBCUs are leading institutions in awarding baccalaureate degrees to black students in life sciences, physical sciences, mathematics, and engineering.
- HBCUs continue to rank high in terms of the proportion of graduates who pursue and complete graduate and professional training.
- Fifty percent (50%) of black faculty in traditional white research universities received their bachelor's degrees at an HBCU.

Chapter 2

Graduation Rates of African Americans attending HBCUs and PWIs

Dr. T. Andrus

According to the Journal of Blacks in Higher Education (2014), the highest Black student graduation rate at the HBCUs included in our survey is at Spelman College in Atlanta. There, 69 percent of entering students graduate from Spelman within six years. The Black student graduation rate at Howard University is 65 percent. This ranks Howard second among the HBCUs in our survey. Hampton University in Virginia ranks third with a Black student graduation rate of 59 percent.

In fourth place is Morehouse College in Atlanta. There, 55 percent of entering Black students earn a degree at Morehouse within six years. The only other HBCUs in our survey with a Black student graduation rate of more than 50 percent is Fisk University in Nashville. Fisk has a Black student graduation rate of 52 percent. At half the HBCUs in our survey, the Black student graduation rate is 34 percent or lower. There are seven HBCUs in our survey where less than one in five entering Black students earn a bachelor's degree within six years.

The lowest Black student graduation rate is at Texas Southern University. There, only 12 percent of entering students earn their degree within six years. In most cases the graduation rates shown here are four-year averages for Black students who entered a particular college or university from 2004 to 2007 and earned their degree at the same institution within six years.

There are a plethora of reasons why some student's do not graduate! Many students stop attending college for various reasons which include: Death, Illnesses, Marriage, Divorce, employment, life changes etc... and the list goes on and on. Despite these types of data our focus should still be on the success of HBCUs to graduate African American Students. As stated previously HBCUs account for only three percent of America's colleges and universities yet they manage to graduate approximately 20% of African Americans. One fifth of all African American graduates earn their degrees from HBCUs. Therefore HBCUs must continue to be protected and funded because HBCUs are the real lifeblood of higher learning for African Americans in the United States.

Make no mistake about it, graduations rates are indicators of whether or not students are sustainable at various colleges and universities. The data below from the Journal of Blacks in Education paints a picture of how African Americans fare in their pursuits of education at predominately white college and universities. These statistics are sobering and shows the great need to keep HBCUS funded and flowing.

Black enrollments in higher education are at an all-time high. But nationwide the black student college graduation rate remains dismally low, at a level of about 45 percent according to the U.S. Department of Education and the Journal of Blacks in Education. The black student college graduation rate is about 20 percentage points lower than the rate for whites. There are many reasons for the low college graduation rate of African Americans and the large black-white gap in college completions:

• Clearly, the racial climate at some colleges and universities can affect black persistence and graduation rates. If black students do not feel welcome or if they experience any sort of racial harassment or discrimination, they will likely drop out of that particular institution. While many of them move on to other schools some students never attempt to regain admission into other schools.

• Many black students who enroll in college are not adequately prepared for college-level curriculum. Poor preparation in K-12 education leaves many black students without a sufficient academic foundation to succeed in college. Poor grades then lead to frustration which increases the likelihood that these students will drop out. Therefore it is paramount that student receive better training in K-12 classes. In this new age of technology more emphasis has to be placed on making sure that all students are prepared for the next chapter of education whether they are college bound or not.

• Many black students come from families that have no tradition of higher education. There can be a lack of necessary support and understanding for nurturing the black student's effort to succeed in higher education. Many African American students enrolled in HBCUs are first generation students. Many of their parents are not familiar with how college structures are set up nor are they acquainted with financial aid, scholarships, housing, support systems etc. Therefore they cannot offer much support to their children or grandchildren who decide to enroll in college.

• But, undoubtedly, the most important factor is money. Research has shown that two thirds (66%) of all blacks who drop out of college do so for financial reasons. Many black students decide they do not want to build up large debts. Others see financial aid awards reduced after their first year in school and do not want to assume additional expenses. At times, increases in tuition, fees, and the price of textbooks push the cost of education too high for black students. Some black students drop out because they need to enter the work force to help support their families. Others who have tried to work while going to college find that undertaking both tasks simultaneously is too difficult and, so, many of these students will drop out of college. Money is without a doubt the number one reason that students drop out of college regardless of race, education level or social status. As America roll out new programs, tuition reductions, financial incentives the forecast for college completions seems brighter. In 2015 the Obama Administration has toyed with the idea of providing the first two years of college free for students who maintain certain academic standards. The United States Department of Education and many regional accreditation agencies have backed various methods of attaining college credits such as credit for prior learning, service learning, CLEP, DANTES, Corporate Training, Challenge Exams etc. All of these innovative ways of acquiring credits helps to reduce the cost of education for many students.

Given the importance of higher education relative to future earnings and career prospects, it is necessary for college-bound black students to have as much information as possible concerning their chances of success at particular colleges and universities.

Graduation Rates of Blacks at HBCUs and Predominately White Institutions (PWIs)

Some colleges and universities have been rated among the best academically in the nation for eliminating the racial gap in graduation rates. In 2008 Grinnell College in Iowa, Smith College in Massachusetts, and Wake Forest University in North Carolina all had a black student graduation rate that was *higher* than the school's graduation rate for white students. At Wellesley, the highly rated women's college in Massachusetts, black and white students graduate at the same high rate of 92 percent. That in itself is impressive!

At several other top-rated colleges and universities, including Harvard, Vanderbilt, and Davidson, the black student graduation rate is very high and is only one percentage point below the rate for whites.

But these high-ranking colleges and universities enroll only a tiny percentage of African-American college students. Therefore, it is useful to examine where black students do well, compared to their white peers, in graduating from the nation's thousands of colleges and universities that are not rated among the academically top tier institutions. It is most important that college-bound black students know of the colleges and universities where their African-American peers have not done so well in completing their bachelor's degree programs. For all college-bound blacks it is important to know where they stand a good chance of success and where they are more likely to fail. Whether we want to admit it openly or not as we face the end of the Obama Administration, the current racial climate in America which has seen uprisings, protest over the shooting of unarmed black men, civil discontentment and calls for racial justice, we realize that Jim Crow is not dead in America and all African American students are not embraced and welcome on all campuses. Therefore it is imperative that African American students know about the success and failure rates of their peers so that they can make intelligent decisions as to where they attend college. It is very hard to study when you return to your dorm room and expletives are written on your door making you feel unwelcomed or a noose is hung in the lobby or on a tree at your campus.

The vast majority of the colleges and universities have racial gaps in graduation rates that are in the range of the national averages. There are actually dozens of colleges and universities where black students actually graduate at higher rates than do white students and there are many more colleges and universities nationwide where the black student graduation rate is the same as the rate for white students.

According to the U.S. Department of Education's website, the widest racial gap in graduation rates in favor of blacks occurs at Southern Vermont College in Bennington. There, the black graduation rate of 56 percent is 23 percentage points higher than the rate for white students. But this good news is diminished by the fact that there are only about 25 black students enrolled at the college.

At Pine Manor College in Chestnut Hill, Massachusetts, the black student graduation rate is 56 percent. This is 16 percentage points higher than the rate for whites. But at Pine Manor, unlike the situation at Southern Vermont College, there are large numbers of black students who are enrolled. Blacks make up 41 percent of the undergraduate enrollments at Pine Manor College. Clearly, the large percentage of black students on campus makes Pine Manor a welcome place for African Americans. This undoubtedly is a factor in the high retention and graduation rates. Correlations such as these are hard to ignore. The more welcoming and friendly colleges are toward blacks the better their chances for graduation!

According to the Journal on Blacks in Higher Education (JBHE) there are 15 colleges and universities where the black student graduation rate is at least 10 percentage points higher than the rate for white students. At some of these schools there are very few black students. But at schools such as Kennesaw State University, Stony Brook University, and the State University of

New York at Old Westbury, blacks make up significant percentages of the student body, and they graduate at a rate that is at least 10 percentage points higher than white students.

There are another 21 colleges and universities where the black student graduation rate is at least 5 percentage points higher than the rate for whites. In this group there are several schools with large numbers of black students. These include Georgia State University, Winthrop University, and Agnes Scott College. Blacks make up at least 20 percent of the total enrollments at these schools.

According to JBHE there are more than 100 colleges and universities where blacks graduate at a rate equal to or higher than whites. Of particular note are those schools where blacks have not only eliminated the racial gap but also graduate at a rate of 75 percent or more. This is 30 percentage points higher than the national average. These schools with high black student graduation rates and where the racial gaps in graduation rates have been eliminated include Lewis & Clark College, St. Lawrence University, Transylvania University, Centre College, St. Michaels College, Wofford College, Babson College, Elms College, and Gettysburg College.

There are several large state-operated universities where black students graduate at rates equal to or higher than those of whites. These include Florida State University, the University of North Carolina at Greensboro, the University of Maryland Baltimore County, East Carolina University, the University of Albany, and the University of South Florida. At Florida State, the university established the Center for Academic Retention and Enhancement (CARE) program in an effort to boost minority student retention and graduation rates. Under this program, students in public schools near the Florida State campus are recruited as early as the sixth grade. Officials from CARE meet with students and parents and build a relationship. After-school and summer programs are offered to help students prepare for college. For students who decide to go to Florida State, a summer bridge program is available to ease the transition. Once enrolled, CARE assists students by offering tutors. Students who are doing poorly are required to attend tutoring sessions in an effort to improve their grades. About two thirds of all CARE students are African Americans. CARE programs should be a vital part of all HBCUs. With Title III programs and HBCUs set aside grants and funds colleges and universities should work hard to prepare their next generations of students. While we should be able to rely on the local school systems to educate our children programs such as these also help to expose future college students and parents to the structures and systems of higher education which is also very vital in regards to the success of students.

Chapter 3

The Historical Significance of Greek Life Organizations on Historical Black College and University Campuses

Sonya Burnett-Andrus, Ed.D.

College students who attend a historically black college or university and desire to have an engaging college experience often join campus organizations; particularly fraternities and sororities known as Black Greek letter organizations (BGLOs). These organizations have been in existence since the early 1900s (Burnett-Andrus, 2015 Kimbrough, 1997, 2003; McClure, 2006; Ross, 2000). Research shows that due to Greek affiliation, African American students at both historically Black colleges and universities (HBCUs) and predominantly White institutions (PWIs) have been exposed to various leadership roles, opportunities for civic responsibility within and beyond the collegiate environment, and a network of men and women who promote and encourage academic achievement and community service (Harper, 2008; Harper & Harris, 2006; Kimbrough, 1995, 1997; Patton & Bonner, 2001).

In spite of significant research verifying the significant impact of Black Greek letter organizations on the campuses of historically black colleges and universities, Kimbrough (1997) declares that the critical question concerning the relevance of Greek letter organizations on college campuses still exists.

African American fraternities and sororities have played a significant role in the history of Historically Black Colleges and Universities (HBCUs). Although blacks have attended southern black universities since the 1860s, black Greek letter organizations were not established until the early 1900s more than 125 years after the white fraternities began. While the opportunity of pursuing a higher education was obtained, the lack of support could cause many to lose the passion to pursue their dream due to the societal pressures which were prevalent during the time. Thus, history reflects the emergence of the African American fraternities and sororities or Black Greek Letter Organizations (BGLOs).

Alpha Phi Alpha Fraternity, Incorporated was the first Black intercollegiate Greek-letter fraternity. Inspired by the racial oppression that African-American students were experiencing on the campus of Cornell University in the early 1900s, the fraternity was founded on December 4, 1906 at Cornell University in Ithaca, New York. In his book, *The Divine Nine: The History of African American Fraternities and Sororities*, Lawrence C. Ross Jr. writes that "African American students were isolated and segregated from the general student population, resulting in an abysmal African American retention rate." Thus, research reflects in the history of each of the African American fraternities and sororities that a support system as well as commitment to the civil rights movement was the basis of the development of each of these organizations which serves as the foundation today.

Much research has been conducted on the roles of the secret societies of fraternities and sororities. There is a particular interest in relation to the significance of the BGLOs on the campuses of HBCUs. Often perceived as the "life" of the campus along with the other extracurricular organizations, African American fraternities and sororities can and often play a significant role in sustaining the legacy of the HBCU cultural experience assisting in promoting retention and graduation.

African American fraternities and sororities have produces some of the greatest leaders in the country and world. Each organization focuses on developing a bond of brotherhood and sisterhood while maintaining visibility within the community promoting scholarship, civic engagement, leadership, philanthropy.

According to Helen Hororwitz (1987), fraternities and sororities have produced some of academe's most visible college leaders. According to Hughes and Winston (1987), The "Greek experience" is thought to expose students to leadership development exhibited by the excellent role models found within their respective chapters, in which they gain additional leadership experiences and skills within their individual chapters and the larger Greek community. Despite these plaudits, fraternities and sororities have received increasing amounts of negative publicity in recent years, causing many in society, and in higher education specifically, to question the right of these organizations to exist (Childs, 1993; Milloy, 1993).

Defining the significance of Greek life organizations on the campuses of HBCUs requires one to understand the founding principles of which these organizations stand. The nine Black Greek-Letter organizations which make up the National Pan-Hellenic Council consists of Alpha Phi Alpha Fraternity Inc. , Alpha Kappa Alpha Sorority Inc., Kappa Alpha Psi, Fraternity Inc., Omega Psi Phi Fraternity Inc., Delta Sigma Theta Sorority Inc., , Phi Beta Sigma Fraternity Inc., Zeta Phi Beta Sorority Inc., Sigma Gamma Rho Sorority Inc., and Iota Phi Theta.

Alpha Phi Alpha: 1906

Alpha Phi Alpha Fraternity, Incorporated was the first Black intercollegiate Greek-letter fraternity. It was founded on December 4, 1906 at Cornell University in Ithaca, New York. According to the official web site, "The objectives of Alpha Phi Alpha Fraternity, Inc. are to stimulate the ambition of its members; to prepare them for the greatest usefulness in the cause of humanity, freedom, and dignity of the individual; to encourage the highest and noblest form of manhood; and to aid downtrodden humanity in its efforts to achieve higher social, economic, and intellectual status."

Alpha Kappa Alpha Sorority Inc.: 1908

Alpha Kappa Alpha Sorority, Inc. (AKA) is the first Greek letter organization in the United States established by Black college women. Established January 15, 1908 at Howard University, the organization has now grown to a membership of over 170,000, with graduate and undergraduate chapters representing every state and several foreign countries. Alpha Kappa Alpha is a sisterhood composed of women who have consciously chosen this affiliation as a means of self-fulfillment through volunteer service. Alpha Kappa Alpha cultivates and encourages high scholastic and ethical standards; promotes unity and friendship among college women; alleviates problems concerning girls and women; maintains a progressive interest in college life; and serves all mankind..."

Kappa Alpha Psi Fraternity Inc.: 1911

Founded on Jan. 5, 1911, on the campus of Indiana University, Kappa Alpha Psi Fraternity was originally referred to as Kappa Alpha Nu. The name was changed to Kappa Alpha Psi effective April 15, 1915. At this time the fraternity acquired a distinctive Greek letter symbol and Kappa Alpha Psi officially became a Greek letter fraternity. The organization now has over 100,000 members in both alumni and undergraduate chapters across the nation.

Membership in Kappa Alpha Psi is a lifelong dedication to the ideas and lofty purposes of Kappa Alpha Psi, which considers for membership only those aspirants whose personal, social and academic qualifications are acceptable to both the College and Fraternity.

Omega Psi Phi Fraternity Inc.: 1911

Omega Psi Phi Fraternity Inc. is the first African American fraternity founded on the campus of a HBCU. With the assistance of their faculty advisor, three undergraduate students gave birth to this fraternity on Nov. 17, 1911 at Howard University. From the initials of the Greek phrase meaning "friendship is essential to the soul," the name Omega Psi Phi was derived. The phrase was selected as the motto. Manhood, scholarship, perseverance and uplift were adopted as cardinal principles. Omega Psi Phi continues the legacy of its founders in promoting the highest ideals and intellectual development of African American men and strives to attract like-minded men who exhibit these qualities.

Delta Sigma Theta Sorority Inc.: 1913

Delta Sigma Theta Sorority was founded on January 13, 1913 by twenty-two collegiate women at Howard University. These students wanted to use their collective strength to promote academic excellence and to provide assistance to persons in need. The first public act performed by the Delta Founders involved their participation in the Women's Suffrage March in Washington D.C., March 1913. Delta Sigma Theta was incorporated in 1930.

According to the official web site, "The Grand Chapter of Delta Sigma Theta Sorority, Inc. has a membership of over 200,000 predominately African-American, college-educated women. The Sorority currently has 900-plus chapters located in the United States, Tokyo, Japan, Okinawa, Japan, Germany, Bermuda, the Bahamas, Seoul, Korea, and St. Thomas and St Croix in the U.S. Virgin Islands."

Phi Beta Sigma Fraternity: 1914

Phi Beta Sigma Fraternity, Inc., an international organization of college and professional men, was founded on January 9th, 1914 at Howard University on the principles, Brotherhood, Scholarship and Service. These principles are exhibited by the fraternity motto, "Culture for Service and Service for Humanity." "Today, eighty-seven years later, the Fraternity has now established the Phi Beta Sigma Educational Foundation, the Phi Beta Sigma Housing Foundation, the Phi Beta Sigma Federal Credit Union, and the Phi Beta Sigma Charitable Outreach Foundation. Zeta Phi Beta Sorority, Inc., founded in 1920 with the assistance of Phi Beta Sigma, is the sister organization. No other fraternity and sorority is constitutionally bound as Sigma and Zeta.

Zeta Phi Beta Sorority Inc.: 1920

Zeta Phi Beta Sorority was founded on the simple belief that sorority elitism and socializing should not overshadow the real mission for progressive organizations - to address societal mores, ills, prejudices, poverty, and health concerns of the day. Founded January 16, 1920, Zeta began as an idea conceived by five coeds at Howard University in Washington D.C.

According to the official web site, "The purpose of Zeta Phi Beta Sorority is to foster the ideas of service, charity, scholarship, civil and cultural endeavors, sisterhood and finer womanhood. These ideals are reflected in the sorority's national program for which its members and auxiliary groups provide voluntary service to staff, community outreach programs, fund scholarships, support organized charities, and promote legislation for social and civic change."

Sigma Gamma Rho Sorority: 1922

Sigma Gamma Rho Sorority was founded by seven teachers on Nov. 12, 1922, at Butler University. The primary focus was to "help young African American women help others." The sorority was forced to overcome challenges associated with being "the only African-American sorority to be founded at a white institution." In addition, the sorority also formed at a time when the Ku Klux Klan was experiencing a mass comeback. In fact, Indiana, where Butler University is located, was often referred to as "Klan Diana." However, Sigma Gamma Rho Sorority still fought to thrive.

Iota Phi Theta

Iota Phi Theta Fraternity, Inc. is the youngest of the "Divine Nine" Black Greek organizations and the last to be accepted into the National Pan-Hellenic Council. On September 19, 1963, at Morgan State College (now Morgan State University), 12 students founded what is now the nation's fifth largest, predominately African-American social service fraternity: The Iota Phi Theta Fraternity, Incorporated. According to the official web site, "As Iota Phi Theta continues to grow and strengthen, so will its commitment to make meaningful contributions to society in general, with particular emphasis in the African-American community. Throughout America,

Iota Phi Theta has come to represent excellence in all areas. The Fraternity is, and shall forever remain dedicated to its founders' vision of 'Building a Tradition, Not Resting Upon One!'"

The role of African American fraternities and sororities on the campuses of historically black colleges and universities is just as significant today as it was as the inception of Alpha Phi Alpha in 1906. There is a significant need for leadership development, civic engagement, and community in our prospective leaders. When individuals understand the history of which organizations stand, then there is a greater commitment to promoting the sustainability of the legacy.

Chapter 4

HBCUs and Sports – Do Great Athletes Leave HBCUs to gain a better chance of getting drafted into the pros?

Dr. T. Andrus

Athletics has always been a part of the black experience therefore it is no surprise that athletics has, is and will continue to play a very critical role in enrollments at HBCUs. Students today as well as those at the turn of the century in the 1900's have enrolled in college with the illusions of grandeur of one day having a chance to play professional sports despite the reality that only 1.2% of college athletes will ever go pro. Perception and reality are distorted among most college athletes. Many athletes believes that their chances of going pro are significantly increased if they attend large predominantly white universities and whether we agree or not according to statistics in regards to the draft they are right. HBCUs have continued to produce less professional athletes since good athletes begin to flock to PWIs in the mid 60's. HBCUs have a great history of athletics but can HBCUs compete with PWIs in their offerings to athletes in 2015 and beyond? Athletic programs also drives enrollment at many colleges and universities. Students want to attend colleges and universities for the most part that have football teams and having a winning record also helps when it comes to recruiting.

The first black college football game was played in Salisbury, North Carolina in the early 1890's. Football quickly found a home in the Negro colleges. From the cotton fields of the South to the slums of major cities, young black boys dreamed of glory in this newfound game with the only problem being that they couldn't play the sport wherever they wanted because they were not welcomed at predominantly white institutions. So, for more than seventy years, young black college-bound football players flocked to black institutions of higher learning. While the major state institutions allowed only a trickle of black players into their programs, the vast majority of black football players, prior to 1965, played their college careers at historically black schools, under the guidance and tutelage of astute coaches who, with little notoriety or glamour, gave of themselves for their love of the student-athletes and the game. Many of the black athletes prior to 1965 regardless of their talents were limited as to where they would eventually spend their college days. Fast-forward 2015, today if you are young, gifted and black colleges and universities from all over America will offer you scholarships. Today the only color that matters is Green! If you can help generate revenue and win championships the sky is the limit on the accommodations you will receive from colleges and universities.

The CIAA, founded on the campus of Hampton Institute (now Hampton University) in 1912, is the oldest African-American athletic conference in the United States. It was originally known as the Colored Intercollegiate Athletic Association and adopted its current name in December 1950. Founding leaders were Allen Washington and C.H. Williams of Hampton Institute; Ernest J. Marshall of Howard University; George Johnson of Lincoln University, PA ; W.E. Atkins, Charles Frasher, and H.P. Hargrave of Shaw University; and J.W. Barco and J.W. Pierce of Virginia Union University.

Football is actually experiencing a major resurgence after going through a period of decline at many HBCUs in the past decades. Because of the financial exigencies of most HBCUs football which is the mostly costly sport to operate on any college campus began to decline in the 1950's and 60's. Additionally, after 1965 many of the best and brightest African American athletes who would have normally attended HBCUs began to be recruited by majority institutions thereby affecting the enrollment of HBCUs.

In Billy Hawkins's Book " The New Plantation" Black Athletes, College Sports and Predominantly White NCAA Institutions, Hawkins expound on how athletics has robbed the HBCUs of its talent and allowed PWIs to operate in the black on the backs of black athletes by offering them illusions of grandeur and the hopes of playing Major League Sports. In chapter three of his book he talks about being intellectually inferior but physically superior. It is worth giving thought to the idea that some of our young men and women are still viewed as property and are not given the nurture and attention that they need to have a successful life after sports. I have a problem with colleges HBCUs and PWIs that just use student's talents for their programs but place little to no effort on their academic success beyond college. No student black or white should be used to just exploit their talents if there is no genuine concern for their careers beyond their college days.

In Chapter four of Hawkins' book he expounds on Operating in the Black on the back of the Black Athletic Bodies. When we look at the revenue contrasts between the Southeastern Conference, the Big Ten, Southwestern Athletic Conferences and the Mid-Eastern Athletic Conference the picture for black sports on college campuses becomes even more dismal and gloomy. In 2012 the Mid-Eastern Conference realized a total revenue of $445,245.00 after expenses. During the same year the Southwestern Athletic Conference (SWAC) realized a net profit of -258,161. Both of these black conferences had very little or no money to distribute to the schools in their athletic regions. How can a conference compete and stay relevant with little to no money? How can these conferences continue to offer scholarships to the best and brightest student athletics?

On the other hand let's look at two predominantly white conferences and their revenues. The Southeastern Conference (SEC) generated $ 455.8 million dollars after expenses in 2014

47

allowing the conference to distribute 31.2 million dollars to each school in its conference. Additionally the Big 12 conference generated 212 million in revenue after expenses and will distribute an average of 13-15 million dollars to each of its schools. How can black conferences compete with these PWI athletic conferences when it comes to recruiting? PWI conferences offer better exposure, more conveniences, more academic support and excited alumni. The sight of walking into a stadium with 70,000 loud screaming voices backing you up and watching the crowds go wild as you envision yourself running a 99 yard touchdown is a bit much when compared to what's offered at most HBCUs. The spinoff however is much more complex and subliminal in that at HBCUs black student athletes although popular during the sports season are also important and respected during the off season! At HBCUs students are respected everyday not for what they do but for who they are. Students are not treated like mascots who are brought out only during game time! At HBCUs black, white, red and yellow students are respected year round regardless of their athletic abilities and talents! That is part of the uniqueness of attending an HBCU.

Fifty years ago, one could argue that black college football was as competitive as any played in the country. The same sort of debates about how the Negro Leagues stacked up against Major League Baseball could be had about black college football and the big-time university game. Having to grapple with talent that segregation placed in their laps, historically black colleges and universities consistently produced average, great and Hall of Fame-caliber professional athletes who played the game as well as or better than their contemporaries.

But the dawn of integration in the 60's and 70's darkened much of the light seen by athletic departments at historically black colleges and universities. After Southern Cal's Sam "Bam" Cunningham knocked segregated Southern football to its knees in a prime-time game against

Alabama in 1970, the doors began to open for black players at schools across the country. As a result, those institutions, underfunded since their founding's, had no advantage over white schools. Once, HBCUs had enough talent to make up for their lack of resources. Now, the talent is gone but the finances are roughly the same.

Before integration, historically black colleges and universities got top black players. When black athletes from the South became able to stay close to home and play "big time" football, historically black schools entered a new frontier. For decades, they'd had less in terms of facilities, but access to fantastic athletes. Once the athletes had access to the luxury, cushy environments of larger, majority institutions, black schools saw fewer top athletes at their doorsteps.

The past 50 years of the NFL draft makes clear the changes in the football landscape. Between 1967 and 1976, as segregation began to fall, NFL teams selected 443 players from historically black schools. During the next 20 years, 291 players from black colleges were drafted. Only 55 players from black schools have been selected in the past 10 drafts.

In states like Louisiana, Mississippi and Texas, where talent was great, the drop-off was most staggering. Between 1967 and 1976, Southern University, Grambling, Jackson State, Alcorn State, Mississippi Valley State, Texas Southern and Prairie View produced more than 35 NFL draft picks per school. In the past 10 years, those schools had a total of 15 players drafted. This is astounding! Where has the talent gone? We know the answer to this question but based on the earlier stats can we realistically reverse this trend? What will this mean for HBCU athletics in the future? Are athletics on their way out at HBCUs?

Since 1997, two historically black schools have won an NCAA college basketball tournament game other than the play-in game: Coppin State and Hampton. And since 2002, a representative of the Southwestern Athletic Conference (SWAC) or MEAC (the only two Division I conferences comprised entirely of black schools) has been in the play-in game every season. The ability to recruit great athletes will continue to impact the enrollments at HBCUs for many years to come!

Chapter 5

HBCU Hiring Practices: Are We Seeking the Best or Are We Content with Just Hiring the Rest?

Doshie Piper, PhD, University of the Incarnate Word

Georgen Guerrero, PhD, University of the Incarnate Word

Heather Alaniz, MS, Texas Southern University

Vachon Venters, AAS

Introduction

When factoring in the hiring practices at Historically Black Colleges and Universities (HBCUs), there is definitely a lot to be considered when it comes to seeking employment in academia. Founded upon a distinctly stated interest and purpose of educating blacks; today, we have some HBCUs thriving, others struggling, and of course there are those that fall in between the two. So, the questions linger on as to why some HBCUs are destined to fail? Will the current state of HBCUs be improved? Not just from the educational perspectives, but also from the hiring practices, to the leadership, the funding, and the recruitment and retention of faculty and staff? Considerable amounts of research has been conducted, data collected, and even criticisms raised in regards to providing answers and solutions on the subject matter. This chapter attempts to answer these questions.

In attempting to examine the quality of the faculty and staff at Historically Black Colleges and Universities (HBCUs) it would be dismissive not to focus attention on the hiring practices and the many common misconceptions centered on those individuals seeking employment at HBCUs. It is critical to determine if HBCUs human resources (HR) department staff seek to recruit qualified candidates or if they are merely filling vacancies to serve the population that attend these institutions. In examining the role of the faculty member, there are a variety of characteristics at HBCUs that make working at a Historically Black College and University attractive. Applicants consider the historical and current contextual viewpoints that HBCUs operate within the academic environment. HBCUs were established shortly after the Civil War with intentions of offering recently Emancipated slaves and their generational offspring an opportunity to obtain a quality education (Gasman et al., 2007). The idea and cornerstone of educating freed slaves, HBCUs driving philosophy, behind their curricula and public services, was primarily that of an industrial-education (Anderson, 1988). Their primary purpose, it was thought, was to help the newly emancipated slaves gain employment, rather than to disseminate knowledge for its own sake, which arguably was the same purpose of Predominately White Institutions (PWIs) (Drewry & Doermann, 2001).

There are other characteristics that influence the decision making process in seeking employment at a HBCU and they include: the institution's tradition, the rank and tenure process for promotion and advancement, and the expected workload. Many of the educators that work at HBCUs believe in the historical mission in which they were established. Individuals that seek employment at Black institutions generally value and respect the historical mission of Historically Black Colleges and Universities and are willing and eager to continue this tradition.

Although faculty members may have broadened their focus, they still maintain a firm commitment to racial improvement through teaching and mentoring (Gasman et al., 2007). Keeping these same beliefs and perspectives in mind, especially when being applied to hiring practices, this often puts HBCUs at a disadvantage in relations to their white counterparts, not just in terms of values that are deemed most worthy, but also in terms of economics, (Gasman et al., 2007).

HBCUs serve a significant purpose for the U.S. educational system, but their funding, academic resources, and overall budgets are routinely quite limited (Gasman et al., 2007). As a result of these limited budgets, there has been a very common trend in many HBCUs being forced to close their doors permanently. HBCUs represent 3 percent of all institutions of Higher Education (Gasman et al., 2007). However, they are still the leaders in granting undergraduate degrees to African Americans, leaders in granting medical and dental degrees to African Americans, and provide training for approximately three-fourths of all officers in the military (Department of Education, 2005). Thus, employing a diverse faculty at HBCUs is necessary to ensure these institutions remain self-contained and continue to produce highly skilled graduates (Jewell, 2002). There is a need for institutions, that offer higher educational services, to pursue and train a workforce; while at the same instance recruit more racial minority faculty (Daufin, 2001).

It has been argued that HBCUs routinely employ academic faculty who were unable to attain academic appointments at neighboring universities based on individual disparities linked to race, ethnicity, and gender (Jewell, 2002). For some individuals, the basis of this argument is an opportunity for academic employment that would not otherwise be afforded to an appointment in a tenure track position. However, promotions in HBCUs appear to be more equitable and less racially biased. Faculty appointments at HBCUs like their non-HBCU counterparts range from adjunct instructors, to non-tenure track lectures, to tenure track positions that include assistant professors, associate professors and full professors.

Table 1.1: 2011 Faculty by Race and Ethnicity and Status

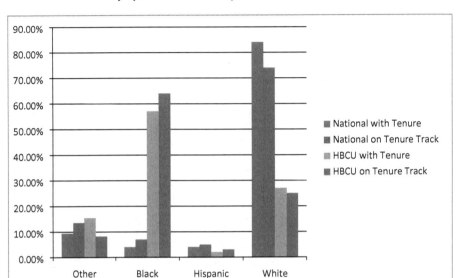

Note: Total tenured or tenure-track faculty at HBCU is 5.694 (NCES, 2011)

In the early 1930s, HBCUs were considered very liberal (Jewell, 2002, & McPherson, 1975). Black colleges attracted faculty that were seeking changes in economic inequality and to explore gender equality, social justice, women's rights, and social equality (Jewell, 2002). From the 1930s to today, many HBCUs continue to employ faculty that foster a liberal societal perspective (Provansik & Shafer, 2004). During the establishment of HBCUs, White women represented a high percentage of the faculty at these institutions as a result of the lack of opportunities afforded females to gain willful employment at Predominately White Institutions (PWI) (McPherson, 1975). As a result, "White professors instructed their Black students in the proper modes of dress, social behavior and religious worship, [and] nearly every HBCU institution employed and enforced strict rules governing the behaviors of its Black student as well as having the curriculum that reflected culture appreciation of the white world" (Jewell, 2002, p. 16).

Foster's (1996) report on the United Negro College Fund (UNCF), from the *Journal of Blacks in Higher Education,* explained that UNCF was primarily funded "by white conservatives and white supremacists who provided financial support to keep Blacks segregated" (pg. 13) and to promote the mediocrity of Black institutions. Foster quotes Sowell's findings, from the *Black Education: Myths and Tragedies,* criticizing the UNCF for condoning and masking the deficiencies of black colleges (pg. 12). The UNCF officially reported that black colleges were doing a good job and whatever deficiencies that they did have could be remedied with more money (Foster, 1996).

Foster in his book *Are Black Colleges Needed, An At Risk/Perspective Guide,* succinctly breaks down this competence and compatibility dilemma:

"During the writing of this guide my eyes were opened to an issue that I had struggled with for many years, particularly in black higher education. How can incompetence be tolerated for so long by persons who know right from wrong but who yet condone egregious administrative ineptitude. During a conversation with someone with whom at one time I greatly respected, I was told that in many black educational institutions, compatibility is much more important than competence and if one must choose between the two, more often than not the person who is compatible with the senior administrator will be hired over the person who is competent. Having known this person for many years, there was absolutely no doubt in my mind that he was totally serious. In spite of the fact that incompetence breeds mediocrity and mediocre institutions produce students unable to compete with their counterparts from more progressive colleges; far too many black colleges try to disguise academic malpractice with rhetoric of excellence" (Foster, 1996, pgs. 1-2).

Despite the fact that a majority of the first HBCUs were dominated by white faculty who lead such institutions based on white cultural principles and practices. With the changing dynamics of the Black student body rejecting being instructed by a predominantly White faculty, the role of diversity needed to be addressed by HBCUs academic administrators. Ironically, minority faculty employed at PWIs found themselves to be socially isolated from the rest of the non-minority faculty due to institutional and individual racism practiced within various academic departments (Daufin, 2001). As a result, a call went out for Black colleges to recruit and retain greater percentages of minority faculty, so HBCUs could develop the practice of hiring minorities and uphold diversity within its academic culture.

Overview of the Hiring Process

Vacancy advertisement or postings for faculty positions varies by institutions and positions. Quite often insider networking and organizational socialization in the profession are the most common ways to advertise a faculty posting. Insider networking for applicants and employees allows for possible vacancy information to be passed to select groups of individuals. Professional or personal recommendations of one individual over another from respected members of the academic community can help and harm prospective candidates. There are many different ways to advertise a vacancy for a faculty position locally, regionally, nationally, and internationally. At the very minimum, most institutions will utilize their human resources (HR) computerized homepages on their respective university websites to announce all faculty vacancies. Even for restricted in-house positions HR must post or advertise the vacant position.

The university's human resources homepage is often the official location to apply for the vacant position regardless of the individual's connection with the university, connections with other employees at the university, or any other association within the faculty or university.

Additionally, vacancy announcements can be promoted through professional organizations, regional and national conferences, and employment websites not associated with the university. Job vacancies can be posted on various listserv, flyers and mailings, at various graduate schools or university departments particularly those with doctoral granting degrees in the respective field that is seeking applicants. Doctoral programs are great locations to advertise job vacancies for doctoral candidates that are nearly completed with their doctoral education; especially those that are classified as A.B.D. (all but dissertation). Doctoral candidates that have received the A.B.D. designation have completed all of the coursework required for the doctoral degree, have passed all of their comprehensive exams (written, oral, or both), completed any portfolio project that is required of them, and only have to complete their doctoral dissertations to complete their doctoral degree. As a result, many of the doctoral candidates that are classified as A.B.D. are prospectively seeking employment opportunities and are interested in learning about potential vacancies in the academic environment.

Once, the position has been properly announced, with the required qualifications and in most cases a list of preferred qualifications listed, through the human resources departmental homepage and applications are received an internal search committee is formed to evaluate potential applicants. The responsibilities of search committees differ by institutions; however for most institutions a search committee is primarily formed to review the applicants' materials. The procedure for applicant evaluation is customarily outlined in the university's faculty handbook. In applying for a faculty vacancy, applicants will generally have to complete and submit an application package that will generally include: a letter of interest, an application, cumulative vitae, a specific number of reference letters or references, and possibly even a writing sample. Again, while procedures vary from institution to institution, some universities may have an individual such as the committee search chair, the departmental chair, a committee member, or in some situations an individual at the university's human resources department to assess what could be a very large number of applications, depending on the number of individuals that apply, and select applicants that meet at the very minimum the required qualifications of the position, as posted in the vacancy announcement. Generally, the person that is conducting the preliminary screening has had previous experience at the rank that the applicant is seeking to gain; however, this is not always the case; such as when a member of the human resources department conducts the initial screening. However, some universities protocols will allow or even require that all committee members to assess the applicants for initial screenings. Once the initial screenings are completed and potential applicants are selected their files will either be forwarded to the hiring committee for evaluation. Based on information provided on the application, CV, letter of interest, letters of reference and the writing sample applicants are selected to continue through the interview process.

Academic institutions are generally defined as either teaching or research establishments; however, there are some technical or training colleges, but generally universities are defined as either teaching or research institutions. Research institutions are generally more research intensive for the faculty members with lighter teaching course loads. Teaching institutions on the other hand, are more teaching intensive and have lighter research requirements for faculty members. During the committee screening process, committees will examine institutional fit between the applicant and the university; research or teaching. This institutional fit will also assist the committee members in deciding if a particular applicant will proceed in the interview process to the initial interview. The initial interview typically consists of a phone interview or a technology assisted interview (Skype or some other face-time software). After the phone interviews are conducted, applicants are again evaluated by the selection committee and based on the applicant's responses on the phone interview they will determine which applicants will continue to proceed through the application process to visit the campus. Search committees will usually have some form of measuring device (a point system) along with lengthy committee discussions that will assist in selecting potential candidates for the campus visit. The top point earners will advance on through the interview process. Generally, only a small number of applicants will be invited for a campus visit. It is not uncommon for this small number of applicants to consist of a single applicant or several applicants. However, this small number is generally around three to five applicants.

During the campus visit the candidates must meet with various university officials including, but not limited to the search committee, the department chair (if not on the committee), the dean, the provost, and the president or someone from the executive council, depending on the particular type of university hierarchal structure, this could be the chancellor or vice president. Applicants at some universities will also meet with a member of human resources to explain the different types of benefit that the university offers their employees. It also allows for the applicant to inquire about the benefits being offered. In addition, if the department has a graduate department, many universities will have the applicant meet with the graduate students as well. This allows the applicant to get a feel for the culture and energy from the graduate programs. Additionally, it allows the graduate students to witness a portion of the hiring process for their own benefit. All of these meetings on campus will generally range anywhere from thirty minutes to an hour with each individual or group of individuals.

While on campus the candidate will instruct a mock class or preforms a classroom presentation. A campus visit can last anywhere from four hours to four days depending on the institution and scheduling. Once the campus visits are complete the committee discusses the results of each candidate and then makes a hiring recommendation to the department chair or dean. If the dean approves the recommendation, it will then be forwarded to the provost. If the provost approves the recommendation, it will then be forwarded to the president. However, if the committee is unable to recommendation any of the applicants to the chair or the dean the search will be considered a failed search. As a result of the usually long hiring process that includes the posting the position, screening the applicants, conducting phone interviews, completing on campus visits and any background work such as calling references once a search has failed it will generally not resume until the next academic semester and very often next academic year. If there is a failed search the process will start all over the following semester or year and repeat until a successful recommendation is made. Once the potential faculty has been selected by the committee then the chair or the dean consults with the provost about the budget and makes the intended faculty member an offer.

Overview of Hiring Process at HBCUs

The hiring process at Historically Black Colleges and Universities, for many different reasons, is not the same process as it is at most Predominately White Institutions. Black institutions lack the resources to adhere to the standard higher education hiring practices. A lack of sufficient resources can affect any number of areas, including personnel, financial, or even equipment, which may result in at least one or several stages of the hiring process may be circumvented. Foster (1996) refers to this practice of awarding positions to specific applicants as a compatibility of competence. "Looking further into this matter of compatibility we find that incompetent persons are often most comfortable with those who are equally as incompetent. Following this line of thinking an equation emerges: incompetence plus incompetence equal compatibility" (Foster, 1996, pg. 2).

A lot of the hiring decisions that are shared among faculty in non-black institutions of higher education are often a single decision at Black institutions. Black college presidents, provost, deans, department chairs and faculty have used a patronage system of awarding jobs to individuals who are compatible with their institutions. To begin to understand the dynamics that influences the decision making process, whether they are covert, overt, direct or indirect upon one another, as the hiring practices are being utilized, one must consider the parallel that has and is being drawn in correlation to the leadership and the faculty.

Research points out that there is a strong disconnect between faculty and administrators at HBCUs and this is likely due to strong opposition towards a one-sided leadership that imposes its prerogatives upon the faculty in relation to institutional government and academic freedom, as noted by Lincoln University professor Robert Millette, who called this phenomenon the "Big Man/Big Woman Syndrome" (Millette, 2005). To-date, one of the most critical areas warranting attention and focus according to Gasman and her colleagues (2007) is that of the faculty roles and involvement in institutional governance and the lack thereof. According to a report from the American Association of University Professors, (2007) that examined the statements on government of colleges and universities, "the primary responsibilities allocated to the faculty are on matters relating to 'curriculum, subject matter and methods of instruction, research, faculty status, and those aspects of student life which relates to the educational process'" (Gasman et al., 2007).

After an in-depth examination of three large well-known doctoral granting HBCUs faculty handbooks from different regions of the United States it was discovered that not a single one of the faculty handbooks outline the hiring process in their respective faculty handbook. Not a single one of the three universities documented the responsibilities of the faculty to screen, interview, or make hiring recommendations. Institutional service work is one-third of the occupational commitment in academia. The work of a search committee should be outlined in the faculty handbook. A quick reference of a Hispanic Serving Institution (HSI) in South Texas found that their faculty handbook outlines the guidelines of a faculty search procedure. This documentation could prove to be extremely beneficial to the faculty who are on a search committee, the applicants, and the university.

In order to learn more about the hiring process at HBCUs a narrative study was utilized to detail the experience of a new PhD recipient in the social sciences. The first example is in reference to a public state run institution in small town in Georgia two hour southwest of Atlanta. The next account will be of the experiences from a private religious liberal arts college in East Texas.

It should be noted that this type of research has limitations. When comparing a narrative study with a single case study Creswell (2007) tends to see the narrative study as more scholarly "because narrative studies tend to focus on a single individual" and allows the information to be presented through the lens of experience (p.77).

Georgia Public School Experience

I remember approaching the data collection portion of the dissertation process. I had already defended my prospectus, during the fall semester, and I knew that I needed to initiate the process for an academic job search. Not knowing much about being on the academic job market, I reached out to my dissertation committee, inquiring about the availability of jobs and the hiring process. One of my dissertation committee members immediately responded to my inquiry with "I know a place where you would do well". Trusting this individual's judgment, I did not worry about the possibility of being unemployed and did not pursue any other academic positions.

I returned my attention to my academic pursuits, completing my dissertation, presenting at national conferences, and getting prepared for graduation. While I was attending the Academy of Criminal Justice Sciences National Conference, I was introduced to a Departmental Chair by one of my dissertation committee members. During the introduction my committee member was making references to previous conversations about my scholastic abilities and achievements; specifically stating "this is my student the one who you are going to be working with". Of course, I was excited; as I thought I had a job, despite the fact that I had not even applied. The feeling did not last long, the Department Chair informed me of where to go to apply online and once I had submitted my application what would be the next step in the hiring process. As instructed, I submitted the application and all of the supporting documents online. I notified the Chair once I had completed the application process. I was immediately contacted by email with an invitation to participate in a campus interview without a phone interview.

Approximately one month later I scheduled my campus interview to Georgia, which just happened to be during the summer. I was responsible for the expenses to and from the interview in Georgia with the knowledge that I would be reimbursed for my travel expenses. The interview was a two day interview. I was provided with an interview itinerary for the two days. The evening I arrived, I had dinner with the Chair of the department, which is standard during a campus interview. At non-HBCUs dinner generally consist of more than one person from the committee. However, I have experienced both single member dinners and multiple member dinners. The following morning I was picked up from the hotel to have a meeting with the Chair over an unplanned breakfast. Following this unplanned breakfast meeting, I had a meeting with the search committee where only one committee member was present.

Upon completion of the meeting, I was expected to conduct a presentation with the entire faculty that was present in the department during the summer before summer sessions begin. The overall attendance for this presentation was extremely minimal. Once I completed the presentation, the Chair and I had lunch on campus at the university dining hall. After lunch I had a series of meetings with the Dean of Sciences and Health Professions, followed by a Dean's meeting, and then the Vice President for Academic Affairs. Towards the end of the day, the Chair and I had a private debriefing where we discussed our experiences from throughout the day. As we talked openly I was provided an opportunity to ask any and all questions in relation to the university, the hiring process, or just questions in general before departing for the airport. After the campus interview, I immediately followed up with a thank you email. The Chair replied with a complimentary email noting that I should "hear something soon". I was offered the position a week later. The official offer came from the Department Chair, but the offer letter came from the Dean of Sciences and Health Professions.

Texas Private School Experience

I heard about the Criminal Justice Assistant professor position online through a listserv where I am a member. I personally knew the Department Chair of the university department that was advertising the position. I called him to get more information about the position. The phone conversation was informative, he was persuasive, and I eventually applied for the posted Criminal Justice position. I went to the human resources website to apply and followed the application process instructions. After applying, I was contacted by phone to schedule a phone interview. The phone interview was with various faculty members from the Criminal Justice Department. The interview went well. Following the interview I was contacted to participate in a campus interview with the executive cabinet.

I attended the interview with the cabinet in the spring semester. I drove to the campus on the morning of the interview. My interview was scheduled for 10am. I met with the Department Chair briefly for about 30 minutes and then we walked over to human resources. I briefly met with a human resources generalist to discuss the various benefits that were available. Upon completion I was escorted to a waiting area outside of a meeting room, where I waited for about 30 more minutes. A Vice President emerged very apologetic, invited me into the meeting room to begin a panel interview. Once the interview was over, I met with the Chair for a lunch meeting. At lunch we discussed the interview questions that were asked and why they were asked. We also discussed the requirements and expectations of the position and my possible transition to the university. I returned home following the very short and brief interview. In the end, I ultimately withdrew my candidacy, in large part, because I was offered and accepted a position at another institution.

What is Being Done to Diversify Applicants?

To champion diversity among HBCUs, the university would need to be more reflective of diversity for both the faculty and student body. Jewell (2002) posits, that "with diversity on both the student and faculty levels came problems with managing diversity both inside and outside the classroom" (p.16). Further, Jewell 2002 suggests that the "prominent role of middle-class whites in the founding of HBCUs often led to the biases of this culturally dominant majority being reflected in the culture and curriculum of these institutions" (p.16). Due to HBCUs academic administration seeking to advocate diversity within its institutions, HBCUs increasingly became the main organizations employing Black academic professionals (McPherson, 1975).

Many HBCUs must convert their hiring practice by embracing diversity, so minority faculty no longer continue to be underrepresented in black colleges (Jacobson, 2003). Gasman (2012) indicated that many HBCU college presidents have publically announced that their college embraces diversity in the 2012 academic applicant pool. In detail, various HBCUs which post academic faculty job positions on the higheredjobs.com website include clauses indicating that the university encourages applicants to apply who will enrich the diversity of the campus community are strongly encouraged to apply (Gasman, 2012). Academic advocates maintain that if the hiring cabinets add diversity clauses to university job positions, these clauses will encourage more qualified minority staff to apply to the university (Gasman, 2012). Further, academic advocates agree that by enhancing diversity clauses to job positions such a mechanism will strengthen the HBCUs historical mission, which champions diversity (Gasman, 2012, Painter, 2000).

Gasman , et al (2007) pointed out that, although faculty at HBCUs have become more diverse, they tend to be less collegial than those at PWIs, where many faculty (most whom are

66

white come from similar racial, ethic, and socioeconomic groups). Not to say there is not diversity at PWIs, but such homogeneity does and can foster easier communication in group settings along with more effective participation. However, when it comes to HBCUs the picture is starkly different, data suggest (Gasman et al, 2007) that the racial makeup is sometimes split between blacks and whites, and these groups are occasionally in conflict.

Research indicates that HBCUs recruit faculty members from diverse racial and ethnic backgrounds (Provansik & Shafer, 2004; Jewell, 2002; & Wilson, 2000). In 2004, Provansik & Shafer found that the faculty employed at Howard University, Atlanta University, and Straight College consisted of Native American, White, Asian, African American, Latino, and Caribbean ethnic backgrounds. In an effort to expand diversity and employment opportunities, President of Frisk University, Dr. Johnson implemented "The International Program of Race Relations, a part of the institute, recruiting faculty from countries in Africa, Asia, and the Caribbean" (Jewell, 2002, p.14). The overall purpose of this program was to ensure that HBCUs maintain the progress of recruiting diverse candidates.

HBCUs are constantly reminded of their inception and the need to create a culture climate that consists of diversity on behalf of the staff and student body (Jewell, 2002 & Wilson, 1995). Inspiring to the educational environment of HBCU organizations is the "behaviors, both overt and covert, of Black faculty, administrators, and students toward White faculty and students as other and representative of the dominant external culture within the majority environment of the Black institution" (Foster 2001, p. 617). Although Black colleges make an effort to recruit diverse minority candidates to secure academic appointments, there is a lack of qualified minority candidates to fill these positions (Foster, 2001). Like most academic colleges,

Black colleges must also meet the academic board accreditation which governs academic institutions.

In 2012, Gasman found that many HBUCs located in Texas have been recruiting more Latino and Asian faculties to work on college campuses. Moreover, Gasman (2012) suggests that "many founders of HBCUs were white and today many black colleges continue to hire white administrators, white staff, white faculty, and enroll a high percentage of white students" (p.2). Gasman (2012) goes on to further posit that different than PWIs, HBCUs do not have a legacy of exclusion and discrimination. Rather, HBCUs have always been open to enrolling and hiring individuals from a multiplicity of diverse racial and ethnic backgrounds (Gasman, 2012).

Daufin (2001) postulate that Black colleges must increase the percentage of minority faculty because minority faculty have validated their superior ability to teach, train, and prepare students for real world life experiences within the work force. Particularly, Daufin (2001) contends that Black college should employee minority faculty because minority faculty contributes to student diversity. Daufin (2001) found that after the passage of the EEO Equal Employment Opportunity Act, Blacks and Latinos made up a small proportion of faculty in academia. Further, Daufin (2001), in his research suggests that minority faculty steer away from academia due to covert racism in tenure and promotions.

Faculty at HBCUs

According to Foster (2001), since accreditation necessitate that a percentage of faculty hold terminal degrees, many HBCUs find it hard to meet those accreditations standards. Many of these schools continue to depend on the "services of White faculty, who had aligned themselves with these institutions for various religious, social, and political reasons, to meet the accrediting standards for advanced prepared faculty members" (Foster 2001, p.619). This suggests that there are White faculty members working in HBCUs which hold tenure-track positions because these individuals simply hold Doctoral degree at higher percentages than minority groups.

White or Caucasian Faculty

Foster (2001) found that in some Black colleges, White faculty has been replaced by Black faculty. Yet, the White faulty that have been replaced by Black faculty members depends on the academic program. It has been established that many Black schools that do not have a high percentage of graduate programs, seek to have a higher percentage of Black faculties on staff than white faculty (Foster, 2001). This is due to the fact that colleges that lack graduate programs are only required to retain faculty who hold a Master's degree as opposed to a Doctorate degree. Many of the HBCUs that retain Black faculty at greater percentages conversely offer academic degrees consist with associates and bachelor level degrees or technical certificates (Foster, 2001). Schneider (1999) reported that five White faculty members sued an HBCU for practicing racial discrimination within the tenure process.

In addition, Black institutions of higher learning across the nation "educate 300,000 students and employ over 14,000 faculty members" (Gasman et al., 2007). Thus there is an urge for HBCUs to recruit and retain an academic staff which is diversified enough to educate the population for which these institution educate (Gasman, 2012).

Black or African American Faculty

In 2001, 58% of the nation's HBCUs faculty were Black and predominantly male (Daufin, 2001). In 1993, 43% of females held academic positions at various HBCUs (Heard & Bing, 1993). There still remains an underrepresentation of Black faculty within academia associated with the lack of Black mentors to guide and inspire minority individuals to pursue careers in academia (Gabbidon et al., 2002, Wilson, 1995, & Healy, 1996). Heard and Bing (1993) research predicted that if the percentage of Black faculty were to increase in academia, colleges essential shall provide positive experiences for minority faculty were they are not exposed to racism as well as sexism. Daufin (2001) reported that in a study with "more than 400 Black faculty; over half of them said they thought that the promotion and tenure process at their institutions was racially biased" (p.19). Overall, the proportion of minority faculty has remained steady at Black schools since 1979 (Daufin, 2001).

Hispanic/Latino Faculty

Black and Hispanic faculty within higher education institutions make up a proportionally small 2 and 3 percent (Daufin, 2001). Altbach (1991) found that Blacks and Latinos often report overt racism as being the most significant barrier to faculty employment. He goes on to explain that in academia, covert racism is often masked by an adherence to a mythical academic meritocracy regarding professional qualifications that subtly favors whites. This covert, institutional or structural racism is based on the notion that the academy was created on a model valuing white homogeneity over diversity (Daufin, 2001).

Minority faculty especially Blacks and Latinos hold academic positions at less prestigious colleges (Daufin, 2001). In a faculty poll at various HBCUs, effects of racism were reported by various racial and ethnic groups (Daufin, 2001). The poll indicated that 70% of Black faculty reported experiencing racism at some point; while employed at an HBCU (Daufin, 2001). In the same poll 51% of Latino faculty and 41% of Asian faculty reported the same experience (Daufin, 2001). Paradoxically, Black schools may abstain Black faculty from experiencing racial isolation but not from institutionalized racism or sexism because Black colleges were founded on the identical assimilationist principles as PWIs (Daufin, 2001).

Positions and Salaries at Black Institutions

Gasman et al., (2007) indicate that HBCUs starting pay for a first year associate professor is much lower than the salary of the same starting position of PWIs. The first year starting salary of an associate professor at an HBCU with 0-2 years of experience is about $7,000 - $10,000 less than the average starting salary for an associate professor with similar credentials at a PWI in the same field (Gasman et al., 2007). Although historically Black colleges were created to educate and give minority students a chance at access to higher education, the research indicates that Black colleges do not employee a high percentage of minority faculties (Gasman et al., 2007, Gasman, 2012, & Foster, 1996). Rather, Black colleges employee White faculty and Foreign faculty at greater percentages than any other racial or ethnic category (Gasman et al., 2012).

Summary and Conclusion

If HBCUs continue to enroll and employ individuals from diverse backgrounds such opportunities will expose these individuals to different ethnic cultures; while at the same time provide opportunities for learning as well as mutual respect (Gasman, 2012). President Obama in 2010 suggested that it was the responsibility of the Department of Education to assist colleges to retain more minority faculty (Kelderman, 2010). As a response to Obama's educational endeavors, the federal government put 1 billion dollars of grant money to aid minority serving organizations to improve in areas like preparation, administration, endowment, and faculty development (Kelderman, 2010).

71

Chapter 6

Open Admission vs. Selective Admission at HBCUs

Dr. Tracy Andrus

Can HBCUs afford to dismantle open admissions at historically black colleges and universities? The answer is a definitive NO! While a century has passed since the establishment of most HBCUs the mission of the HBCUs are still the same and that is too educate African Americans which also include those who may not be adequately prepared to enroll in mainstream education courses. According to the National Center for Education Statistics (NCES) African American Males enroll in the highest number of remedial courses in their first year of college. In recent years colleges and universities in at least thirty states have begun outsourcing remedial education to outside agencies and community colleges. Without open admissions many students (black, white, Hispanic, etc.) would not be able to attend four year colleges period.

Because HBCUs are charged with the mission of educating the prepared and underprepared masses of African American and others who enroll in their colleges and universities it is paramount that open admissions remain a part of these institutions. Some people may comment that if students did not do well in high school how are they expected to do well in college? Good question but the answer is not always so simple given the fact that many students are not placed on the college curriculum trajectory in high school. Parents, counselors and teachers don't always instruct students on how important it is to take particular course that would better prepare them for entrance in college thus allowing the students to take the easy way out.

According to IPEDS and the U.S. Department of Education one out of every 10 Black males who are enrolled in college attends an HBCU. This research suggest that HBCU graduates enjoy greater financial success in their careers, and U.S. rankings consistently show that HBCUs are among the top producers of students who continue their educations through graduate and professional schools. However, there are many social factors that disrupt the best efforts to recruit, retain and graduate Black college students.

Systemic inequities and racial biases within schools systems are contribute to Black being overrepresented in the colleges with open admissions standards, including community colleges and for-profit colleges, and underrepresented at colleges and universities with selective admissions standards, including many HBCUs. Today, of the 1.2 million Black males currently enrolled in college, more than 529,000 (43 percent) are attending community colleges, compared to only 11 percent who attend HBCUs. Another 11 percent of Black males attend for-profit universities, such as the University of Phoenix, which as a single institution enrolls the largest number of Black males in the nation.

In the current educational environment, even our most gifted Black males with the most dedicated parents can leave high school underprepared. Often, students with very low GPA, low ACT/SAT scores, and key math and science classes omitted, have difficulty gaining acceptance to traditional 4-year institutions. This trend seems to be expanding each year. More and more we see traditional four year institutions public and private, HBCUs and PWIs becoming more selective in who they are allowing to enroll in their institutions.

73

According to NCES, approximately 258,047 of the 4.1 million ninth graders in the United States are Black males. Among them, about 23,000 are receiving special education services, and for nearly 46,000, a health care professional or school official has told them that they have at least one disability. If Black male ninth graders follow current trends, about half (50%) of them will not graduate with their current ninth grade class, about 20 percent will reach the age of 25 without obtaining a high school diploma or GED, 45 percent of Black males will attempt college, however only 16 percent obtain a bachelor's degree by the age of 25. These are starling statistics that are very sobering but realistic based on data trends.

According to the Department of Education's 2012 *Civil Rights Data Collection* report opportunity gaps that exist between Black and White males across the country center around three key areas: (1) Schools routinely offer Black children a less rigorous curriculum that omit classes required for college admission; (2) Schools discipline Black males more harshly by suspending them for behaviors (e.g. tardiness) that rarely result in suspensions among White males; and (3) Black students are the most likely to have the lowest paid teachers with the fewest years of classroom experience, and who become teachers through alternative teacher certification programs. This report is critical in light of who is teaching our children? Questions must be asked but most importantly actions must be taken to offer a more challenging curriculum for African American students that are college bound school discipline must be more consistent for all students regardless of race or class and teacher pay and experience must be equally distributed in all school districts. This is an action item that must be address all over America.

According to recent research most Black males persist through high school and aspire to attend college at rates that exceed White and Hispanic males. In a national survey conducted by the U.S. Department of Education, National Center for Education Statistics, 87 percent of Black students who were in the 9th grade in 2009 were in the 11th grade by 2012. In addition, Black students were more likely to advance ahead than fall behind or drop out. About 64 percent of Black high school males expect to eventually graduate from college. However, Black students are behind their peers in the percent who are taking college preparatory classes. Fifty-three percent of Asian students, 24 percent of White students, 16 percent of Hispanic students, and 12 percent of Black students are taking pre-calculus or calculus by the 11th grade. As a result of these trends African Americans entering college are underprepared for most math and science classes.

HBCUs and open access to all students

HBCUs have the potential to play a major role in expanding college access to all students seeking admission into college. However, HBCUs need coordinated and proactive strategies to disrupt a system that underprepares Blacks for postsecondary education and restricts their higher education options to the least competitive institutions of higher education. HBCU leaders should be active in crafting policy solutions for HBCUs to resolve inequities in U.S. public schools that impede academic progress of African Americans. HBCU students can change the public perception that school-age Blacks are disaffected and incapable of adapting to the educational system. HBCU academic affairs administrators can promote a pathway through AP classes that can help Blacks transition from public schools to colleges and universities. Through teacher education programs and trainings, HBCUs can examine the impact of teacher preparation on the academic achievement of Blacks and aid in breaking the discipline gap barrier in our nation's schools. HBCUs must become more proactive in helping to establish curriculums that will benefit college track students.

In February 2014, President Obama launched **My Brother's Keeper** – a new initiative to help every boy and young man of color break barriers and get ahead. The initiative surveys and builds on the work of communities and institutions that are adopting approaches to promote success among males of color. Many HBCUs have initiatives that can contribute to the national agenda to help Black males to reach their full potential, contribute to their communities and build successful lives for themselves and their families.

The White House Initiative on HBCUs (WHIHBCUs) will work with the HBCU community and the Interagency Task Force that will oversee My Brother's Keeper to do the following:

- Use research and programs published by HBCU scholars to recommend Federal policies, regulations, and programs that would benefit boys and young men of color and innovative strategies and practices for providing opportunities to and improving lives for Black males.
- Survey HBCU male initiatives to contribute to the administration-wide "What Works" online portal to disseminate successful programs and practices that improve outcomes for boys and young men of color.
- Confer with HBCU researchers and administrators to recommend critical indicators of life outcomes for boys and young men of color for a comprehensive public website, to be maintained by the Department of Education.
- Connect HBCU administrators and scholars to the philanthropic and corporate partners of My Brother's Keeper so that they can learn how to access the revenue necessary to start and sustain programs for boys and young men of color.

To achieve these objectives, in February 2014, the WHIHBCUs began a series of sessions to bring together students, educators, policymakers and other interested in the advancement of

Black males to discuss key policies and strategies for increasing their college preparation, recruitment, retention and graduation. The goal is to promote the academic success of Black males at HBCUs through leadership, scholarship and civic engagement.

Every year thousands of students have the opportunity to attend college because of open enrollment. Dictionary.com says open admission is a policy of admitting applicants to an institution, especially a university, regardless of previous academic record or grades.

The policy creates equal opportunity for the rich, the middle class and the "have-nots," to get an education. Historically black Paul Quinn College in Dallas, Texas got rid of its open admissions policy and saw retention rates shoot up from about 60 or 65 percent to 83 percent and was named the "2011 HBCU of the Year" among other awards and recognition. Other HBCUs have also questioned their open admissions policy.

If HBCUs have stood the test of time by serving disproportionate shares of low-income students, can our much-loved institutions really afford to lose more black youths today if open admission is no longer present? If not HBCUs then Who? If we do not give our young men and women a chance to earn a college education then who will? We see the trends in higher education and we know that the elephant is in the room and that is why we must stand steadfast and do our best to improve student's academic preparations coming out of high school and fight to dismantle barriers that would prevent them from being able to obtain a college education. In the words of Forest Long "A Mind is a terrible thing to waste".

Chapter 7

Why are Historically Black Colleges and Universities Declining?

A Historical Overview

Julian L. Scott, III, Ph.D.

Georgen Guerrero, Ph.D.

"How we have arrived at the present state of affairs can be understood only by studying the forces effective in the development of Negro education since it was systematically undertaken immediately after Emancipation. To point out merely the defects as they appear today will be of little benefit to the present and future generations. These things must be viewed in their historic setting. The conditions of today have been determined by what has taken place in the past, and in a careful study of this history we may see more clearly the great theatre of events in which the Negro has played a part." – Carter G. Woodson, 1933

Historically Black Colleges and Universities (HBCUs) were established shortly after the American Civil War with the intent of providing an education to Emancipated slaves. Prior to the Civil War only a handful of blacks had graduated from an academic institution with a college degree; the very first being Alexander L. Twilight in 1823 (Bennett, 1988); however he graduated from a white institution. As a result, in 1865, the Freedman's Bureau began to establish black colleges and universities throughout the northeastern portion of the United States. The most notable university being Cheyney University (originally known as the Institute for Colored Youth); as it is recognized as the first Black College to be established in the United States in Cheyney, Pennsylvania in 1837 (U.S. Dept. of Education, 1991). Shortly thereafter, Lincoln University in Pennsylvania (1854) and Wilberforce University (1856) were both established also before the Civil War.

Religious organizations such as the African Methodist Episcopal Church (along with Baptist, United Methodist, and Presbyterian churches) sought to secure land and buildings to establish early private black colleges and universities. The Reconstruction Era revealed shifts in national politics and progressively charted the course for the abundance of African American representation primarily from the Southern States. As a result, the importance of educating African Americans became evident (Williamson, 2008). Subsequently, these institutions were called universities or "institutes" since their inception, a major part of the mission of the HBCU in the early years were to provide elementary and secondary education to students that did not have any education.

The passage of Morrill Act of 1890 saw the emergence of the black land grant institutions for the establishment of A&M (Agriculture & Mechanical) schools. Several major universities such as: Southern University, Prairie View, and North Carolina A&T (formerly known as North Carolina A&I) were supported by the passage of the Morrill Act (Thompson, 1973; Gasman, 2007). These institutions were established in southern or Border States which ultimately came under public control (Dept. of Education, 1991). Williamson (2008) acknowledges that the passage of the Morrill Act of 1890 was designed to satisfy the demands and ambitions of Northern industrialist. However, the most fundamental principle of the Act was to provide land grant institution specifically for blacks; yet place these institutions deep within the confines of rural areas that had the highest concentration of blacks (John, 1920). Booker T. Washington, President of Tuskegee Institute, supported the notion of a thorough vocational education. W.E.B. Dubois was at odds with the "accomodationist" attitude of Washington toward white philanthropist, yet the underlying focus of Booker T. Washington's industrial education curriculum was to provide early African American college students with the skills needed to fit a bifurcated means to an end: employability in factories and the ability to create entrepreneurship through the mastery of agriculture science and skilled trades.

It was not until 1900 that HBCU's began offering courses and programs at a post-secondary level. With the support of *Plessy vs. Ferguson* in the recent 1896 "separate but equal" ruling blacks were educated privately in HBCUs. J.D. Rockefeller, John F. Peabody, and Julius Rosenwald had provided substantial amounts of money to erect buildings and other infrastructural to provide black land grant institutions with the support needed to provide a surplus of skilled black labor black labor to meet the industrial needs of the American economy.

Prior to 1915, in what became a national debate, curriculums at historically black colleges and universities focused more on industrial education than liberal arts curriculum. The debate focused around the idea that blacks should be educated to fit the needs and appreciation of the upper class elites by educating them towards skilled or technical employment. Many of the early institutions hired white faculty to instruct the curriculum at HBCUs. Black students were taught proper dress attire, appropriate social behavior, and religious worship from white faculty (Jewell, 2002). Historically black colleges and universities began to integrate the liberal arts curriculums into the existent industrial model (Williams, 2008). The integration of the models made it possible for the earliest graduates of historically black colleges to go into depressed, rural areas that needed teachers to provide an education to the children of sharecroppers and sharecroppers themselves.

Today, many HBCU's have residents halls that carry the name Peabody Hall, Rockefeller Hall, and Rosenwald Hall. On a personal note, one of the authors of this chapter is a graduate of Fort Valley State University and during his undergraduate years he succinctly remembered one the institutions finer facilities carrying the name, "Peabody Hall." Moreover, the philanthropic contributions to historically black colleges and universities were needed and proved valuable; however, the journey of the historically black college was a long arduous process. Consequently, this placed blacks at a disadvantage because they were separated from Predominately White Institutions (PWIs) of learning.

The first quarter of the 20th century through legal litigation saw the creation of law schools, medical schools, and other professional schools based upon the ideology set forth by *Plessy v. Ferguson* (1896). During segregation *Missouri ex rel. Gaines v. Canada* (1938), *Sipuel v. Board of Regents of University of Oklahoma* (1948), *Sweatt v. Painter* (1950), and *Sanders v. Ellington* (1968) saw the creation of graduate programs, in particular, law and medical schools at historically black colleges and universities. The law and medical schools created at black colleges and universities proved to produce some of the nation's best and brightest physicians, lawyers, and judges. It was not until the landmark case *Brown vs. the Board of Education of Topeka* was decided in 1954, which allowed for the integration of students, that blacks started to increase their numbers at Predominately White Institutions. Prior to Brown 90% of black students received their education at a HBCU; that number dropped drastically to 17% as of 1996.

Integration began to usher new challenges that would ultimately affect the longevity of historically black colleges. *U.S. v. Fordice* (1992) was integral in the attempt to level the playing field for black colleges (Wertz & Conrad, 2002). Although, the aforementioned court cases proved victorious for historically black colleges various state legislatures acted slowly with regard to providing funding that was as equivalent to their respective flagship institutions. The lethargies of State legislatures stymied the progress of historically black colleges and universities while giving predominately white universities an economic advantage through the unbalanced appropriation of funding to specific institutions of higher learning.

81

In 1989, President George H.W. Bush issued Executive Order 12677 to strengthen the capacity of historically black colleges and universities to ensure that those enrolled would receive a quality education by widening each respective school, faculty, and student participation in federally sponsored programs. Additionally, the bill required that the private sector provided some assistance to historically black colleges and universities. The Executive Order is administered through the Office of Postsecondary education; moreover, 27 federal departments were selected for participation in the program because they accounted for 98 percent of federal funding directed to assist historically black colleges and universities (Department of Education, 1991). Accordingly, the State of the Union Address (2015) outlined a plan that would make the cost of community college virtually free; however, if HBCU's do not adopt pertinent marketing models that aggressively recruit individuals post community college they will lose to the predominately white universities that are planning or have already engaged in articulation agreements with 2 year community colleges or technical colleges as DeVry Institute. To offset a potential crisis HBCU's may have to consider articulation agreements with other HBCU's based on specific programs and creating a pipeline to sustain graduate programs across curriculums. Either way, the HBCU's will be faced with considerable challenges to remain competitive, yet offset paltry enrollment numbers to remain competitive.

Despite the challenges that historically black colleges have faced and overcome they played a vital role in providing equal opportunity for an education for all students. As noted by the Department of Education in 1991:

- Approximately 80% of all black Americans that receive training in medicine and dentistry attended Howard University or Meharry Medical College.

- HBCU's have provided training for at least three fourths of all black persons that hold doctoral degrees.

- HBCU's are the leading institutions in awarding black student baccalaureate degrees in the area of life sciences, physical sciences, mathematics, and engineering.

- HBCU's continue to rank high in terms of the proportion of graduates who pursue and complete graduate and professional training (Dept. of Education, 1991).

Additionally,

- As of 2005, approximately 19.7% of all black Americans still receive training in medicine and dentistry attended Howard University or Meharry Medical College.

- As of 2005, HBCU's have provided training for three-fourths of all black officers in the armed forces and four-fifths of all black federal judges (Dept. of Education, 2005).

In contrast, historically black colleges and universities have suffered disproportionately in comparison to their Predominately White Institutions (PWI) counterparts. There are a variety of issues that negatively affect these institutions. Largely, because historically black colleges and universities have been actively committed to serving students that are from disadvantaged backgrounds as well as the history of underfunding and discrimination. Paltry budgets, a dependence on federal funding, limited revenues, questionable administrative practices, and low enrollment numbers have forced leadership within historically black colleges and universities to make tough decisions to keep their institutions marketable and at the same time keep them afloat (Gasman, 2014). In a desperate attempt to save their schools, several universities from various states have even adopted the practice of recruiting students from other races to help maintain minimal budgets (Sum, Light, and King, 2004)

In 1967, the *Harvard Educational Review* published an article entitled "The American Negro College" by Christopher Jencks and David Reisman in 1967 that garnered a plethora of attention from both the academic community and the press. The authors considered the HBCU's to be academic disaster areas which damaged the reputation of HBCU's across the country. The language within the article, coupled with the social climate of the late 1960s, and the push toward integration coerced many academic leaders to question the relevance of HBCU in a post segregation society. The landmark ruling in *Brown vs. Board of Education in Topeka et al.*, that outlawed segregation, influenced several parties to wonder if historically black colleges and universities were even needed. Although this was not the only piece of academic literature written to assess the quality of education at HBCU's, yet around the 1950's so called "concerned" parties began to question the kind of education that was taking place at HBCU's (Jones, 1969).

Marybeth Gasman's (2006) article *Salvaging "Academic Disaster Areas": The Black College Response to Christopher Jencks and David Reisman's 1967 Harvard Educational Review Article* examined the detrimental effect that Jencks and Reisman (1967) caused to the image of HBCU's, especially, within the popular press. Gasman's (2006) commentary had revealed a bias against historically black colleges. In fact, Jencks and Reisman (1967) did not produce valid data as a means to substantiate the following claims levied against HBCU's: 1) the lack of understanding of the HBCU community, 2) false institutional comparisons, 3) dismissal of the contributions of black leadership, 4) use of anecdotal evidence, and 5) the lack of scientific rigor to substantiate claim that HBCU's were indeed failing and needed to be removed from the realms of higher education. Gasman (2006) further alluded to the inflammatory nature in which the article was structured and written; however, despite the argumentative flaws pertaining to the research and methodological design the article was accepted by Harvard University. Perhaps then the misguidedness of white scholars when making negative references to the academic rigor of the HBCU's, the quality of professors, and the leadership of administration was widely accepted by leaders in the field of higher education and competing predominately white

84

institutions. The portrayal of HBCU's as disaster areas proved not only erroneous, but it revealed that greater mainstream society did not truly understand the educational plight of HBCUs, nor did they take into consideration the practices of State legislatures that decide the areas in which HBCU's were allocated funding; not only sustain these universities, but improve the quality of life for those that attend and work at HBCU's. Oftentimes, scholars whose perceptions of the HBCU's were in the vein of Jencks and Reisman (1967) had neglected to explain that all HBCU's were not the same.

In refuting such claims of Jencks and Reisman (1967) C. Shelby Rooks, of The Fund for Theological Education, took issue of the negative characterization of HBCU's by noting:

> Despite unconstructive criticisms and the lack of adequate resources the [Black colleges] do much more than give their students "an idea of what middle class life is like." The truth is that the vast majority of Negroes who achieve success in American life were educated in this "academic disaster area." (Rooks, 1967, p.19).

To further substantiate the statement by Rooks (1967), Bohr et. al. (1995) revealed that students that attend historically black colleges tend to achieve academically because of the supportive environments that are offered to students. Davis (1994), further noted, that black men that entered an HBCU with lower grades and SAT scores outperformed their peers at predominantly white institution that entered college with higher grades and higher Scholastic Aptitude Test (SAT) scores. Bohr et. al. (1995) noted that African Americans felt academically and socially isolated at predominantly white universities. Gasman (2006) and Bohr et. al. (1995) subconsciously formulated a particular question - If blacks are to attend a predominantly white university would they still have been better off? It could be easily argued that the answer would be, not necessarily. The warm and welcoming environment for a black student at a historically black college and university may not be felt at a predominately white institution. Each institution

85

regardless of its PWI, HBCU or Hispanic Serving Institution (HSI) status develops internal strategies for students to succeed at their respective schools. These strategies attempt to focus on developing an appropriate plan for the genetic make-up of the student body. It could be easily argued that an HBCU would have a better understanding of what African American would need to be successful at a HBCU verses a PWI that is serving black students at a PWI. The same could be argued for a Hispanic Serving Institution attempting to provide for Hispanics and also for a PWI that is attempting to provide an education to white students. It could easily be argued that each school understands their own racial and ethnic cultures better than those outside of that racial and ethnic background. The literature is filled with research that describes the alienation, discrimination, and social isolation that blacks feel at Predominately White Institutions.

Historically black colleges and universities have overcome a fair share of their obstacles over a period of time, but they are now confronted with an ever changing higher education market place. The growing competition among HBCU's and predominately white universities are forcing HBCU's to revisit their strategic efforts as it relates to institutional infrastructure, recruitment/retention, accessibility to broader urban market (Association of Governing Boards, 2014). HBCU's must implement strategies needed to recruit a more diverse student population. Very few HBCU's have attempted to create programs that attract students from countries abroad. As more and more students are coming to the United States to obtain a college degree, the international market is worth adding to any recruitment activities.

Furthermore, despite the recent growth of on-line programs across the United States and elsewhere there have been a limited number of on-line programs being developed at HBCUs. As a result of the growing number of non-traditional students at universities and the accessibility to everyday use of the internet HBCUs should attempt to break into this potential pool of students, as recommendation by Penn and Gabbidon (2007) in their examination of HBCUs. They also recommend the hiring of visiting professors to enhance the cultural mix of faculty (Penn and Gabbidon, 2007) and not just the students. The use of the visiting faculty member could help with the recruitment of a more diverse student population.

The decline in HBCU's is attributed to the notion that HBCU's are erroneously considered to be inferior to their predominantly white counterparts. Scholars in the field of higher education quickly recuse themselves from challenging the standard of living and life afforded to black students and understanding that this can have a drastic effect their success at the university level. Although history has shown that HBCU's graduate dynamic leaders that serve in many facets of society they lag behind or are under engaged in areas related to enrollment, management, and marketing (abg.org, 2014). African American students receive a quality education at HBCU's yet the reason for the decline in HBCU's lies primarily on the shoulders of the various institutions lack of revealing their excellence to mainstream society and the false misrepresentation of white scholars painting the worst picture of HBCU's to students of various backgrounds that are misinformed.

Accordingly, there have been several closures of historically black colleges as a result of failures in leadership, financial mismanagement, and inadequate levels of institutional effectiveness. Recent closures of HBCUs include Morris Brown College in 2013, St. Paul's College in 2013, Bishop College in 1988, Mississippi Industrial College in 1982, Daniel Pane College in 1979, and Kittrell College in 1975. Though it may be painful to bear, the recent closures of Morris Brown College or St. Paul College, to say the least, warns other historically black colleges and universities that they must adapt, change radically, and develop strategies that would continue to keep them relevant in the 21st century (Chesley, 2013).

Financial Instability

The decline of support in public institutions is waning yet historically black colleges and universities must explore ways to remain fiscally stable. Without adequate funding these universities are in danger of becoming obsolete. Financial stability is a major part of continuing the accreditation of the Southern Association of Colleges and Schools (SACS). Moreover, if a university is failing in the area of fiscal management, SACS has the right to deny accreditation; especially, if they have been continually cited by the accreditation body in this area.

Gasman & Bowman (2011) alluded to the fact that historically black colleges and universities have failed to adequately address the importance of giving. Executive leaderships at HBCU's have segregated the large donors from the small donors creating a philanthropic vacuum. This ideology of isolating and classifying donors is dangerous. When we are trying to help universities that are struggling to survive every dollar, quarter, nickel, dime, and penny is significant despite the stature of the donor. Segregating givers might insinuate to the small donor that their contributions are insignificant. Consequently, these individuals may respond to such separation, by asking to be removed from the pool of donors. It is possible that a collective body of smaller donors might cast a negative image on the college when conversing with potential recruits, reclaimed alumni, and those wanting to give, but had not found the appropriate institution to donate their respective monetary gift. Therefore, it is imperative to hold on to as many donors as possible regardless of the donation amounts. Even if they lose the larger donors, institutions are able to argue that their institutions are widely donated when the sheer volume of donors is higher with several smaller donors verses having only one large donor. Most important, Bowman (2011) exclaimed: "Alumni giving starts with students. We need to start teaching students about giving back while they are still on campus instead of waiting until they are alumni and are easily distracted by life." Historically black colleges and universities have historically fallen by the wayside in terms of their fundraising operations. Gasman & Bowmen (2011) note that historically black colleges lag behind because they have failed to develop the following strategies:

- The failure to promote and cultivate future fundraisers by not introducing student that has an interest in philanthropy. Meaning, historically black colleges need to hire fundraisers of color that understand the historically black college environment and the needs of its alumni.

- Historically black colleges and universities have failed to promote giving starting as early as freshman orientation, new student orientation, and transfer student orientations. Stakeholders at historically black colleges and universities must encourage the parents of the students to get involved in the giving process.

- Historically black colleges and universities must strengthen relationships with community organizations, foundations, and other funders to create opportunities for creative and innovative thinking.

- Historically black colleges and universities must keep abreast of the changing agendas of private funders and make connections with those agendas. Historically black colleges and universities must show funders how they plan to respond and lead major trends that affect higher education.

Historically black colleges and universities have smaller endowments than predominately white institutions, in large part, because throughout the establishment of historically black colleges and universities they have received less funding on the state and federal level. Second, alumni's giving is at best significantly weak because African Americans historic lack of wealth has stemmed from economic exclusion. However, historically black colleges and universities must rise to the challenge with regard to fundraising. Historically, black colleges have erroneously made the assumption that alumni have little to give and doubt that the return on their investment has value. Many historically black colleges and universities have taken such drastic steps as employing reductions in force, coercing staff and faculty member to take unpaid furloughs, and cut funding for activities that promote the student's well-being (Gasman, 2014).

The recruiting of visiting faculty could help HBCUs financially with the teaching of courses at slightly discounted prices. As faculty are taking furloughs or paid sabbaticals from their home universities, HBCUs could reap the benefits of having a full-time full-professors teach for a year or semester at a lower salary. Since many faculty are still being remunerated, usually at lower salaries, from their home universities during their sabbaticals, HBCUs would not be required or expected to offer full salaries to visiting professors.

Gasman (2009) found that fundraising efforts post the *Brown* era substantially began to decrease because the historically black colleges and universities were deemed as substandard as compared to predominately white institutions. The assumption among liberal and foundation leaders was that historically black colleges and universities would no longer be in existence. Consequently, historically black colleges began to suffer economically during the first few years after *Brown* (Gasman, 2007; Trent, 1981). By the early 1970s, 31 private black colleges were operating at deficits that totaled nearly 7.5 million dollars; six United Negro College Fund (UNCF) colleges either broke even or had a minimal surplus (Trent, 1971; Holsendolph, 1971; Thompson, 1973). Many college and universities have had to furlough or release faculty and staff to help reach the minimal financial levels needed just to remain operational ((Burke, 2013). Unfortunately many historically black colleges and universities will have to officially close their doors as a result of their inability to stay afloat financially (Burke, 2013). Scholarship dedicated to philanthropy have paid attention to the relationships among white philanthropist and the degree in which they support black institutions; however, very scant research has been performed to assess the nature, in which, historically black colleges raised monies on their own behalf (Cutlip, 1965).

Gasman (2007) and Gasman & Anderson-Thompkins (2003) examined how the impact of the black consciousness movement effected the procurement of donors for the purpose of giving. The lack of scholarship makes it difficult to understand the practices that are best suitable to formulate new strategies or modify existing strategies with regard to fundraising. Even more problematic to historically black colleges and universities was the fact that foundations began to give more money to stronger institutions rather than those that they considered weak institutions (Thompson, 1973). Institutions that had a decreasing student body, with decreases in enrollment did not generate the interest in donors to assist the failing institution. The American Council on Education (1969) noted that the federal government was not sympathetic to black colleges. Many historically black colleges had to redirect their funding from student related programs or even worse downsizing the number of faculty at the institution to meet the requirements for federally matched funding programs. Moreover, the discrepancies between funding historically black colleges and universities and predominately white universities were evident; however, historically black colleges and universities would not have survived without the assistance of indirect and direct federal funding programs. Ninety percent of students at historically black colleges and universities receive financial aid according to the data presented by the U.S. Department of Education's Integrated Postsecondary Education data system. One part of the financial crisis effecting historically black colleges and universities is the mission of historically black colleges and universities; which are to a) provide access to marginalized populations and b) historically black colleges and universities cannot afford to alienate the communities and people that they intend to assist.

Drops in enrollments could cause withdrawals of endowments or matched funds can create dire consequences for historically black colleges and universities. Currently, without the assistance from donors or the lack of outreach to potential donors historically black colleges and universities will steadily lag behind. Colleges and universities with bigger endowments and federal aid packages will recruit and gain those talented students that historically black colleges and universities are targeting. To further add insult to injury in the recurring cycle of giving, these students that are recruited away from HBCUs to other universities could very well go on to be successful in their own right; allow them to donate back to their alma maters, which are no longer HBCUs that they were originally recruited to and are in dire need of any and all donations. Therefore, it is imperative that historically black colleges create and recreate their methods with regard to creating a healthy financial position. It is important to remember that for some minority students the rewarding of a financial package through scholarships from their university they will not be able to attend college. In 2013, over 16,000 students at HBCUs were forced to find funding from alternate sources or withdraw from school altogether when they were not able to obtain federal aid (Mullins, 2013). Additionally, the universities were these students were not able to return lost millions of dollars in revenues (Mullins, 2013)

Leadership Styles and the Presidential Carousel

Keeping the most qualified candidates that apply or are considered to be worthy candidates at historically black colleges and universities are daunting tasks. Presidents at historically black colleges and universities make substantially less money than those presidents that lead regional and flagship predominately white institutions. Unfortunately, as a result, many individuals will accept employment at a Historically Black College or University as a mere stepping stool to gain experience and then will move on to other institutions. Many presidents that take posts at historically black colleges bring a wealth of academic experience, a mastery of teaching, and the ability to perform the highest quality of research given their respective disciplines. However, Gasman (2011) found stereotypes, of historically black college presidents, have foreshadowed the realities and the complexities that they must overcome.

> Gunnar Myrdal (1944) wrote: "Negro leaders more often than whites (among their own people take on a rather dictatorial and paternalistic attitude toward their Negro followers. They seem to mimic, in a smaller degree the role of the upper class white Southerner in his relation to his dependents....The organization of life in the Negro colleges seems to be definitely less democratic than white colleges in America, even, and not least, when the staff of teachers is mainly Negro. The president in his relations to the professors and they in their relations to the students act more dictatorially and more arbitrarily" (p. 732-733).

To further extend the ideologies of Myrdal (1944); Ralph Ellison (1952) classic work

Invisible Man complicates the matter more in terms of the ideologies of the dictatorial character

Bledsoe:

> "Negroes don't control this school or much of anything else...nor white folk either. True the 'support' it, but I control it. I's big and black and I say 'yes, suh' as loudly as any burrhead when it is convenient, but I'm still the king down here. I don't care how it appears otherwise....Let the Negroes snicker and the crackers laugh! Those are the facts, son. The only ones I even pretend to please are *big* white folk, and even those I control more than they control me" (p. 142).

Contrarily, Jencks & Reisman, (1967) although scathingly criticized historically black

colleges they did acknowledge the difficulties faced by black college leaders:

> "While there were plenty of president Bledsoes in the Negro colleges there were also courageous and progressive men who did much more than most college presidents, they had to depend on the weapons of the weak: guile and rhetoric and seeming compliance. Without such men, however, the years of complete segregation would have been more stifling than they were, for by drawing on their connections with cosmopolitan whites they were able to create at least some breathing space in the Negro community" (p. 18)

Thomas Sowell (1973) remarks the following with regard to the perception of black

leadership at historically black colleges and universities by his statement:

> "The tragic irony is that there are already-at this moment- enough competent black scholars and able black students in the United States to create several good black colleges. But we are unlikely to have been put in key positions-where they do their job

93

badly, but they create an atmosphere which repels people who are so desperately needed" (p.304)

The leadership styles of historically black college and university presidents have great bearing on the faculty of those respective institutions. Conversely, there are two important concepts that have been adapted based upon the German conceptualization of academic freedom: 1) *Lehrfreiheit*-the professors' right to research and 2) *Lernfreiheit*- the students' right to study what he or she pleased. The American Association of University Professors (1915) set forth the guidelines to ensure that the college professor have both the freedom within the classroom, freedom to research, and publish on the concepts of his or her choice. Faculty members at historically black colleges and universities often times feel that they are limited with regards to academic freedom. In retrospect, historically black colleges and universities were supported by white industrial philanthropist whose primary concern was to keep the HBCUs burdened of coercing its earliest students to become enamored in a vocational learning environment than a liberal arts curriculum similar to that of predominate white institutions (Anderson, 1980). The curtailment curriculums found that historically educational leaders were purposely coercing historically black colleges and universities into maintaining curriculums that would easily provoke criticism, yet keep historically black colleges and universities from fully competing with predominately white institutions.

John D. Rockefeller established the General Education Board during the 1920's with the intent of industrialist as a means to monopolize the underdeveloped status of black higher education to suit the needs of industry. For example, Gasman (2014) provides a glaring example of how the need for support from donors outweighs academic freedom. Gasman (2014) explained the story of Lee Lorch. Lorch, was white, yet he was a strong proponent of educational and equal rights for students at Fisk University during the 1950s. However, President Charles

Johnson was concerned that Lorch's activism would create a stir among white philanthropist; although, these philanthropist were staunch segregationist. Lorch's activism placed considerable pressure on Robert Johnson and it ultimately led to his dismissal from Fisk.

During the early, 1970s Eddie Paul Wendt and Chuck Ballas, the first White students to attend Prairie View A&M University, were enthralled in a heated battle to allow students that attended Prairie View A&M the right to vote. In 1979, U.S. v. Leroy Symm, Waller, Co. the Supreme Court held that Prairie View A&M students should not be denied the right to vote in Waller County simply because they were college students. Unfortunately, those student trailblazers were either dismissed from the university or left on their own free will (Charleston, 2014). The failure that lay in both of these examples are that money and politics makes for strange bedfellows especially; when there are interest that seek to mute the much needed development that would allow for progressive action and thinking that would advance the agendas of historically black colleges and universities.

In reality, faculty, staff, and students complain, yet they do not understand the struggles and the challenges that presidents of historically black colleges and universities must endure. Many historically black colleges and university presidents must be quick to listen and slow to react based upon the audiences that they need to address. Historically, both private and public black college and university experience different, yet similar challenges (Gasman, 2011). Presidents of private historically black colleges and universities might have more latitude than those presidents that preside at publically funded historically black colleges and universities. Possibly then, the conflicting nature of leadership within black colleges is fraught with internal campus politics that involve faculty, students, and boards of trustees. Gasman (2012) examined the presidential vacancies at historically black colleges and universities. The major concern was the exorbitant number of presidential vacancies that have occurred. Gasman (2012) highlighted the fact that the departures might be attributed to various reasons; including, the stress of the economy and the public's ability to pay for higher education. Most importantly, historically black colleges and universities have been unable to provide the amenities and immense resources that predominately white universities have been able to accumulate over the years. Consequently, Boards of trustees must be criticized for lacking three most important elements that are needed to choose the appropriate leader for a university: 1) knowledge base 2) skill base, and 3) a resource base.

Additional scholars have analyzed the issue of presidential vacancies by comparing the employment practices at historically black colleges and universities to the national football league. The conclusion gave the perception that historically black colleges and universities rewarded mediocrity rather than achievement. What has become very problematic; meaning, there have been occasions where a historically black college president has been fired for lack of performance, yet reappears at another black institution. Furthermore, when they do arrive at their new university, they will arrive with more experience; thus having the ability to demand more pay. Having a high ranking administrator absorbing large portions of the fiscal budget at struggling institutions can weaken struggling budgets even more. Additionally, this revolving door of presidential leadership does not allow for proper development of strategic goals at these universities. It is erroneous to assume that historically black colleges and universities cannot retain the proper leadership for each distinct institution, yet one might argue that a good ol' boy system can be adequately applied to how historically black college presidents employ individuals to key positions that are a part of personal networks. Although, the claim might appear to be anecdotal in nature; data might reveal stark suggestions that friendships have taken over the business, instead of, hiring the most appropriate individual to move the business agendas of historically black colleges and universities forward to meet the challenges of the ever-changing processes occurring within higher education. Consequently, these and other challenges that affect historically black colleges and universities have been ignored. Historically black colleges and universities like all universities need people that are great leaders and not just good managers.

During the commencement address at Fisk University in 1924, DuBois openly criticized the anomalies pertaining to historically black colleges and universities presidents cautionary stance against educated blacks desire to seek and maintain autonomy by stating the following:

"I have come to address you and, I say frankly, I have come to criticize...I come to defend two theses, and the first is this: of all these essentials that make an institution of learning, money is the least. The second is this: The alumni of Fisk University are and if right ought to be, the ultimate source of authority in the policy and government of this institution...Fisk University is not taking an honest position with regard to the Southern situation. It has deliberately embraced a propaganda which discredits all of the hard work which the forward looking fighters for Negro freedom have been doing....It continually teaches its students and constituency that this liberal white South is in ascendency and that it is ruling and that the only thing required of the black man is acquiescence and submission."

Lastly, historically black colleges and universities have traversed many boundaries that have been tumultuous at best. However, the resilience shown by the leadership and students provides a glimmer of hope for the future. The failure that looms over historically black colleges can be view as partially self-inflicted and non-self-inflicted. In order, to meet the demands of the 21st century historically black colleges and universities must take charge of their respective institutions through entities as fundraising, retention, presidential leadership, and encouraging innovative ideas that allow academic freedom to faculty members. Historically black colleges and universities are more scrutinized a bit more than predominately white institutions; however, the significance of historically black colleges and universities contributions to the American landscape is not only vital to the successes of the African American community but mainstream America. Currently there are 106 historically black colleges and universities in the United States including two year institutions, four year institutions, public institutions, private institutions, graduate schools, medical schools and law schools. A few of the more identifiable historically black colleges and universities include: Tuskegee University in Tuskegee, Alabama, Xavier University in New Orleans, Louisiana, Spelman College and Morehouse College both residing in Atlanta, Georgia, Hampton University in Hampton, Virginia, Florida A&M University in Tallahassee, Florida, Prairie View A&M University in Prairie View, Texas, Alabama A&M in Normal, Alabama, Howard University in Washington D.C., and Lincoln University in Lincoln University, Pennsylvania. These are only a small handful of the many historically black colleges and universities across this nation that have maintained their commitment, not only to the African-American community, but to American community in their pursuit of achieving educational equality across all racial and ethnic communities.

Opponents of historically black colleges and universities have adamantly proclaimed the institutions as being a fixture of the past and should be rendered obsolete. In hindsight, if it were not for historically black colleges approach to educating people regardless of color and social class America would have lost a substantial number of individuals, with regard, to the contributions being made in every field of human endeavor. Most important, we must understand that historically black colleges were not institutional despots that were seeking handouts, but institutions that worked with very little yet made tremendous gains. We should be reminded of this touching, yet factual story that resonate the power of the historically black college:

During the 1930's a young chorale instructor received an appointment to teach music at Prairie View A&M University. Her name was Bessie Patterson. Bessie, was accompanied by her brother named Frederick and they both made the long journey to Texas. Frederick was age 13; however, while running errands and performing odd jobs- he met Dr. E.B. Evans, professor of Biology and Animal Sciences. The mentorship taught Fredrick the value of hard work, learning by doing, and sacrifice. The moral of this story- Dr. Frederick Patterson, not only became the president of Tuskegee Institute but he also established the United Negro College Fund. In reflection, when one of the co-authors of this chapter would get tired, weary, or even lethargic; I am always reminded of Dr. E.B. Evans- Professor Emeritus of Biology, Prairie View A&M University most famous moniker to Frederick that is synonymous with the pervasive struggle of the survival of historically black colleges, students, and faculty: "A Mind Is A Terrible Thing To Waste." Please support the United Negro College Fund and historically black colleges and universities because "Black Minds Matter".

Chapter 8

Characteristics of the Top Ten HBCUs In America and Why They Are Continuing to Thrive

Dr. T. Andrus

There is no doubt that there are certain characteristics that are constant at HBCUs that continue to find themselves rank in the top ten year after year. These schools have consistent leadership, they have supporting alumnus, all major sports offered to their students, they have bands, scholarships, great infrastructures, capacity building initiatives with other institutions, competitive tuitions, blends of face to face and online courses, graduate programs including masters and PhDs, very strong and supportive Board of Trustees, excellent community and service programs and are very active in their communities.

These are some of the noted similarities of Historical Black Colleges and Universities that continue to find themselves on the top ten list year after year. These schools have less turnover in their top administrators which can be a plus for most institutions. The longer Presidents, Provosts and Vice Presidents serve an institution the more acquainted they are with the institutions strengths and weaknesses. Presidents who are able to identify and correct minor problems at their institutions gain support of the faculty and staff and secures the vote of confidence needed to tackle larger problems.

Leadership ability is ranked as the number one reason that colleges either thrive or perish regardless of rather they are HBCUs or PWIs. Leadership is key! Therefore presidents must be involved, visible and to a certain degree passive-aggressive in securing resources for the colleges and universities that they serve. While no president can carry the load of the college alone, he or she is seen as the engine that must pulls the rest of the cars and the caboose. If the president is ineffective, dormant and not energized it will soon be reflected in the day to day operations of the schools where they serve.

Successful HBCUs have very supporting Alumnus who eagerly give back. These students graduate with grace! There is nothing more detriment to a school than to have an alumni graduate with an unpleasant experience. Students who graduate with unpleasant experiences do not in many cases contribute financially to their alma maters. Former students play a significant role in sustaining their colleges and universities and they should be sought out to give back to their schools. College graduation is ranked in the top five percentages of being the accomplishment that most people are proud of if they have a college degree. Former students are constantly reminded of their schools when they complete applications for employment, credit, and when they look at sports among other things.

All of the HBCUs that have been ranked in the top ten for the last ten years offer all major sports at their institutions. These institutions have bands, choirs and a plethora of activities to offer to their students. While some relish the idea of concentrating on strictly academics, it is a fact that many students enrolling in college want to either participate in or attend athletic events. The top ranked sport for all of these colleges is football. While basketball is ranked a close second, no other sport draws crowds like football. Attending football games with the college band, cheerleaders and Greek organization representatives brings festive –exhilarating excitement to students like nothing else. On the other hand HBCUs who are ranked at the bottom do not have many sports activities to offer their students and the ones ranked in the bottom 10% do not offer football at their institutions. While some institutions have chosen not to brand their schools with sports being a major catalyst, those schools who have offered full athletic programs seems to have thrived more in the last decade.

Successful HBCUs offer a mixture of scholarships to their students. Colleges and Universities must be able to offer some forms of scholarships to deserving students if they expect to recruit high achieving students. HBCUs are faced with competition from PWIs when it comes to the ability of schools to offer deserving students scholarships. The offices of sponsored programs, financial aid and career planning at the top ranked HBCUs continuously research grants and special scholarships to make them available to deserving students at their institutions. These value added infringements help students to unload debt and make the students work harder toward maintaining high GPAs in an effort for them to retain their monies. Schools that offer less scholarship and grant opportunities to their students normally have lower enrollments and less sustainability with retaining their high achieving academic students.

HBCUs that are ranked in the top ten have great infrastructures to accommodate students, faculty and staff. These institutions have computer labs located in various areas on the campus, meeting/study rooms for students/varieties of eateries/food and snacks to offer to students, extracurricular activity rooms and fields, sprawling relaxation environments, excellent workout facilities and welcoming environments. Many of these institutions have research labs, manicured lawns and are continuously working on capital projects to expand their campuses. As a result of the Office of Civil Rights (OCR) money that was given to certain institutions, these institutions have been able to build structures that will accommodate students for centuries to come.

One of the characteristics that stood out most in this research was the ability of the top ten institutions to collaborate and join other institutions in their capacity building initiatives. Schools who build relationships with other institutions were at a greater advantage to receive the multimillion dollar grants from major donors. While many HBCUs may not offer certain programs nor have certain infrastructures that they need to win certain grants, institutions that have been able to align themselves with other institutions have consistently been able to leverage their abilities to compete by combining their resources. Institutions who forged relationships with other institutions have been much more able to compete for resources than those who have not reached out to other institutions. The same is true for department within the HBCUs. Grantors are looking to get the most out of their money and in many cases recommend that departments work together to accomplish their missions.

The top ranked HBCUs all have competitive tuitions. These schools while having great reputations for graduating top ranked students have kept their tuitions competitive with other local colleges and universities. Colleges who have kept their tuitions competitive and offered great academic programs have continued to thrive in the last decade. While many schools are enrollment driven, these top ranked HBCUs have focused more on selective admissions. While the criteria vary most of these HBCUs have tried to make it possible for the majority of students to enter their schools based on their academic abilities. With the recent changes in financial aid regarding the parent-plus loans and the increase in tuition at many colleges, those colleges who are able to keep their tuitions competitive will continue to reap their rightful share of students in the years to come.

With the new advent in higher education, no school will be able to survive or adequately compete if they do not offer online courses. The paradigm has certainly shifted today as the majority of students coming out of high school are much more in tune with technology. Schools ranked at the top all have this one point in common, they offer online classes. The days of the fifty minute lecture is becoming a dying art in many schools and colleges. Students want to receive rapid information today. Sitting in a class for 50 minutes or one hour and 15 minutes will soon be a thing of the past for most colleges and universities unless the lecture is pre-recorded and able to be uploaded on a device. Colleges and universities that do not offer mixtures of face to face and online courses will find themselves be left behind. While we will cover technology in another chapter, that is why it is paramount that all colleges and universities have excellent technological infrastructures. Failure to be technologically sound will result in disaster for any college or university in the next decade. All colleges whether PWIs or HBCUs have basically one choice either prepare for the onslaught of online education or perish. In the near future even Jr High and High School students will be completing most of their work from home!

Top ranked HBCUs all have graduate programs which includes the offering of masters and PhDs. These institutions of higher learning provide avenues of which their students can attain the highest degrees in their fields. These graduate programs are notable and produce alumni that are able to compete globally as well as abroad. Students who complete these graduate programs work in some of the top research laboratories, engineering firms, best hospitals, and serve as lawmakers, in the senate, congress and other fortune five-hundred companies. HBCUs must continue to thrive to produce more PhDs so that we can have a pool of leaders who will be able to take on the youth of tomorrow.

Another strong characteristic of top-ranked HBCUs is the strength and makeup of the Board of Trustees. All of the top-ranked HBCUs have very strong, engaged, supportive Boards of Trustees. Many of these Board members have served for many years, many are former graduates of the institution at which they serve and all of them have and continue to make great sacrifices for their institution. The board members of these institutions have differing backgrounds but all of them have a special connection to the institutions that they serve. All of the trustees at these institutions bring something special to the table in the form of their expertise, ability to gather resources, philanthropy etc. Colleges and universities depend on their boards of trustees to help guide the institution in the right direction. Board of Trustee Members must therefore be able to give their unbiased opinion on what is in the best interest of the college without fearing any reprisals. The Board of Trustees is the most powerful body of administrators at any college or university in that they make the final decisions to accept the recommendations of the Academic Council and the Cabinet.

Finally, HBCUs that are consistently ranked at the top have excellent community and service programs and are very active in their communities. It goes without saying that colleges and universities must be engaged with the community. Colleges and universities that engage their students and faculty in service projects garner positive exposure from the community which results in positive advertisement for the school and will likely result in the recruiting of students. When colleges sponsor community forums, presentations and activities that engage the community they build relationships with citizens and employers that last for decades.

Chapter 9

HBCU Staff And Support, Can They Get The Job Done?

Dr. T. Andrus

Very few people would disagree with me regarding the fact that HBCUs need their staff support to carry out their missions for the institutions where they serve. The staff and support components of all HBCUs cannot be underestimated in regards to how important staff and support are to HBCUs. Staff and support can be the difference between students staying at a college or university or leaving the institutions. Students often complain about the fact that staff members are not courteous, organized and they do not return phone calls or reply to emails at many HBCUs. All of these concerns involve customer service. Customer service is the lifeblood of any business and institutions of higher education are no exception. Staff should always work to make sure that students do not become frustrated. Often time it will mean that they have to leave their personal problems and situations in the parking lot when they arrive at work. The same is true for presidents, deans, directors, faculty and all other higher institution personnel. We cannot bring our personal problems to work and expect to offer great customer service to our clients which are the students.

The staff at HBCUs are charged with many duties and they wear many hats. Sometimes staff complain about being underpaid and overworked but that in itself should never diminish their propensity to service the student body. Staff are responsible for a plethora of duties and work all over the campus they are responsible for recruiting, admissions, financial aid, business office matters, the registrar's office, student affairs to name a few. Being pleasant to students, faculty and staff must be a constant whether they feel like it or not.

Staff, support and maintenance personnel are really the one that under girt the colleges and universities and in many cases they are the least recognized. When the staff and support personnel work well together HBCUs have much happier student populations. Many students have expressed their concern regarding how staff sometimes pass the buck by sending them from one station to another just to have other staff send them away. This is no doubt frustrating for many students and it makes it appear that we at institutions are not organized. We must do a better job of centralizing our student support services so that students do not have to walk across campus to get business matters taken care of. It would be great to have admissions, financial aid, registrar's office, business office, housing, IT and other offices adjacent to one another so that students can have a one stop shop. Forms and computers should be readily accessible to all students in a centralized location to assist them when needed. HBCUS and PWIs must work to become more student friendly and continue to strive to provide the best customer services to their students. Customer service also drives enrollment.

Our Staff and support personnel are very capable and competent to carry out their jobs and assignments. There is nothing greater to see than staff and support working together to serve our students at HBCUs. Students know when departments and personnel are working together in unison and trying to resolve their matters and they also sense when they are not. Faculty, staff and administrators can get much more accomplished when we all work together and everyone stays in their lanes. Staff and support personnel play a very vital role at HBCUs and their work contributions should never be taken for granted nor diminished by HBCU administrations. Without the staff and support personnel many HBCUs would not be able to exist.

Chapter 10

HBCUs and Technology, Are we still metaphorically operating in the Dark Ages?

Dr. T. Andrus

While many HBCUs are operating with superb technology, there is a call for all HBCUs to get on board and do so in a hurry. Students attending HBCUs today are more inclined to use smartphones, watches, computers and other digital devices. Typewriters, old dinosaur computers and televisions are things of the past. We must meet students where they are in regards to technology. Technology should be integrated in all classroom regardless of the discipline. Interactive technology added to discussion and engagement for students as most students appreciate hands on learning and relevant current events. Integrating the events into the classroom assist professors in many ways and excite students to the point of wanting to attend classes. The day of the 45 minute lecture is over! Technology is here to stay and we must use it more often in our classrooms.

With the advent of online education comes an even greater need for HBCUs to offer superb technical services to its students. Online education in higher education is the wave of the future. As time passes by brick and mortar institutions will become less inhabited and online learning will become increasingly the norm. In our jet-set society many of our daily activities prevent us from having time to attend a brick and mortar institution and many people would rather complete their work assignments at home at their own pace. Furthermore there are some perks of working at home that we all know about but cannot do much about. Online learning opens the door to integrity issues. It is quite possible to have someone complete a degree for another person thereby raising ethical issues. While many colleges and universities are toying with the idea of using biometrics to reduce integrity issues with online learning the fact still remains that we will continue to have hurdles to cross for decades before this problem can be resolved. HBCUs must have reliable servers and equipment to foster a positive learning environment for online learners.

Another point to consider is who is operating our equipment at HBCUs. HBCUs can spend hundreds of thousands of dollars for great technical equipment but if the person running the equipment is not competent the equipment will never work properly. The use of the equipment will only be as good as the person using it. HBCUs must make sure that they are hiring competent technical staff to maintain their databases, servers and technical infrastructure. Colleges and universities cannot operate with the continuous loss of internet services and a lack of competent technical personnel. At the end of the day good servers will result in good service and bad servers will result in bad service. If HBCUs are to remain competent many of them must do a better job of overhauling their campus technology. The question is not can we afford to have great technology? Today at colleges and universities institutions must have great technology or they will perish it is just that simple. Technology is the wave of the future either we grow and move with it or we will certainly get left behind!

To better serve our students, I believe that all HBCUs should provide a free laptop computer for all students entering college whether they are freshmen or transfer students. Additionally, the schools should make sure that their internet infrastructure is superb in all areas and provide students with internet hotspots throughout campus, including the dining hall, dormitories and in various meeting places on campus. With these computers learning will take place 24/7 as professors and students will be able to collaborate with each other at any time from any place.

The use of technology fosters interactive/interdisciplinary learning also among students at HBCUs. The use of paper to write on in the classroom is also becoming obsolete as more students are using their smart pads, computers, phones and other devices to take notes in the classroom. As we become more technologically savvy the death of paper in the classroom becomes more eminent. Technology is definitely here to stay! I envision that in the next five to ten years high schools and Jr. High school attendance will be greatly diminished in lieu of the use of technology. More and more Jr High and High school students will begin using online education to earn their diplomas.

Chapter 11

Territorial Administrators and Why Divisions and Departments Work Against One Another?

Dr. T. Andrus

"Lord if we can ever just get everyone who works at HBCUs to understand that we are on the same team, Lord we would make some sweet music together" Dr. Tracy Andrus. For some reason, it seems like someone did not get the memo that says that we are on the same team! While I know that there are exceptions to all that we say and believe, one thing sticks out farthest and in my opinion has caused the demise of many institutions and that is the division among HBCU's faculty, staff and administrators. Most of us know that we are on the team but we don't understand that we are on the same team. We are not playing against one another we are playing with one another! If we are going to compete, lets compete against other institutions not other departments and divisions within our own schools. Jesus Christ said any house divided against itself cannot stand. Furthermore Father John Dickinson in 1768 stated that united we stand and divided we fall. HBCUs must do a better job of working with each other. The belief permeates throughout most HBCUs that if I can make your department or division look bad then it makes my department or division look good, but in essence we make the college look bad and create tension and animosity among the students, faculty, staff and administrators who in many times are exposed to incidents and altercations.

In the words of Rodney King, Can't we all just get alone? The us against them mentality exhibited by faculty and staff and supported by some administrators will be the doom of many departments, divisions and colleges. There should never be the us against them mentality at no business or organization but for the HBCUs knowing the times that we are living in, this should never be mentioned among us. We should strive to work together as a family. All of our paychecks are tied to the survival of our institutions. If our colleges close down we will all be seeking employment and in many cases this does not have to be if we learn to work together. Once again, it does not matter where we work, we must not allow our personal life circumstances creep into our daily work activities. Faculty, staff and administrator at HBCUs are there to assist the students and make the college or university the best that it can be. This should be the prevailing thought of all of us! Students first! We should not try to make it hard on one another to get things accomplished to show each other up. That mentality only serves to work against and undermine the entire institution. Once again customer service in my opinion is the strongest predictor of determining whether or not an entity will survive or perish!

A great concern among personnel at HBCUs is the Us against Them sagas that play out day to day at many HBCUs. It should never be us against them but always us period. Academic Affairs should never be at odds with student affairs neither should the registrar's office be in conflict with financial aid or the business office. Sometimes it seems that the division that we have at HBCUs are purposely orchestrated to make once area look worse than the other area which eventually leads to finger pointing and the blame game when things go wrong. When we learn that we are all in this together then we will harness our strengths and remove the barriers that prevent us from working together in harmony. We will then understand that we don't have to make other people or divisions look bad so that we can look good. We will then be able to adopt the slogan "If they don't look good, we don't look good".

We must understand that when we compete and negatively undermine each other we work against the progress of the institutions at which we serve. We are not just hurting the other components of the institution but we are hurting our students, academic programs, finances and the college as a whole. Every time we lose a students for whatever reason (lack of organization, poor customer service, failure to process their financial aid in a timely manner, forgot to register them before the 12th class day, failure to challenge them academically, food in the cafeteria, condition of their dorm room, lack of extracurricular activities etc., the college loses revenue. All institutions operate on a forecasted budget. When enrollments projections are not met many institutions are forced to furlough or lay off faculty and staff. Many institutions can change their course by working together and not seeing other area jobs at being mutually exclusive.

Recruiting at any college or university is everybody's job not just admissions. Everyone should be recruiting at their institutions. Departments that reach out to their potential applicants usually have higher enrollments than departments who do not. Working together as a team will always prove beneficial to all involved because we can do much more than we think if we just do it together. In the words of the Late Great Dr. Martin Luther King, "Either we will learn to work together like brothers, or we will all perish like fools"! We have got to get it together and learn to work together because no man is an island and no man or institution will stand alone. Even our Lord and Savior Jesus Christ stated that "A House divided against itself cannot stand". Where there is unity there is strength.

Chapter 12

Financial Aid and HBCUs – Why HBCUs Cannot Survive without Financial Aid

Professor Teresa Francis Divine

Financial Aid Changes and HBCUs

By Teresa Francis Divine[1]

When Barack Obama was elected in 2008, Historical Black Colleges and Universities (HBCU) hoped for a great partnership, a champion for the institutions that have held such significance in the Black community. However, under the Obama Administration, HBCUs have faced challenges with enrollment and retention due to governmental financial aid changes. HBCUs have expressed disappointment and outrage with the Department of Education and the Obama Administration for not considering the effects the changes would have on HBCUs.

The Federal aid changes to the Pell Grant, Parent PLUS Loan and possible sanctions for a high cohort default rate have caused uneasiness for HBCUs. This chapter will discuss the financial aid controversy and its effects on the HBCU community.

Historical Black Colleges and Universities (HBCUs) were established after the abolition of slavery for the express purpose of educating African American people. Over the years, these institutions have educated a great number of Black professionals and community leaders (Barthelemy, 1984).

---

[1] Teresa Francis Divine formerly-(Teresa I. Francis) is an Associate Professor in the Law and Justice Department at Central Washington University.

The creation of Black colleges and universities came about because there were no other opportunities for Blacks to get a quality education. By limiting access to quality education, many Whites hoped to cripple the political aspirations of African Americans and inhibit the ability of Blacks to compete with Whites economically. Some Whites also hoped to insure a low-skilled menial labor force comprised of uneducated Blacks. Early on, education was about literacy and basic math (Williams & Ashley, 2009). Many of the first institutions offered social skills, agricultural skills and other trades (Williams & Ashley, 2009).

According to Albert L. Samuels' book, Is Separate Unequal? Black Colleges and the Challenge to Desegregation, one of the principal concerns among White southerners was the right type of education for the Black race: "Blacks should not aspire to higher education" rather they should be content with vocational training in various trades (Samuels, 2004, P.34). This sentiment was real and was not just in the minds of community members, many state governments passed laws that specifically forbade African Americans from attending White universities (Samuels, 2004).

Thus, African American institutions were separate but facilities were far from equal financially. Black colleges and universities often struggled. Many southern states did not allow Blacks to attend White colleges or universities and the state legislatures in those states appropriated little funds to Black institutions. Samuels (2004) provides the following example: "Louisiana's state constitution limited the annual appropriation to Southern University to $10,000 until 1919" (p.35).

The lack of equal resources was also apparent when Congress authorized the Morrill Act of 1862 and created land grant colleges. As stated in Is Separate Equal? "the act provided that a grant of land to each state be sold with proceeds to be used for the endowment, maintenance, and support of at least one college where the leading object shall be without excluding other scientific and classical studies and including military tactics to teach such branches of learning as related to agriculture, mechanical arts in such a manner as the legislatures of the states may respectively prescribe" (Samuels, 2004, p. 36). State legislatures had exclusive authority to disperse Morrill funds. Most states simply did not allocate the federal land grant monies to institutions whose aim was the education of Black students (Samuels, 2004).

As of 1890, nearly 30 years after the Morrill Act passed, only three states: Mississippi, South Carolina and Virginia, shared money with Black colleges (Samuels, 2004). Congress was prompted to pass a second Morrill Act of 1890 to ensure equitable distribution of funds to benefit both Black and White students. Nevertheless, states routinely denied funding from the Black land grants to Black colleges and universities. When Black schools received land grants funds, it was only a portion of which they were legally entitled (Samuels, 2004, p.37).

In 1965, Congress introduced an institutional aid program for Historical Black Colleges and Universities (20 U.S.C § 1060); it would be the first time HBCUs would be recognized and officially defined. Section 322 of, the Black College and University Act of 1965 defines HBCUs as institutions established prior to 1964 whose principal mission is the education of Black Americans (Samuels, 2004).

Part B of Section 321 of the act asserts that state and federal governments have discriminated against HBCUs by denying financial support under the Morrill Act of 1862. Part B provides financial assistance to establish or strengthen . . . and protect the financial management, academic resources and endowments of the HBCUs ... The act also facilitated a decrease in the reliance on governmental financial support and encouraged reliance on endowments and private sources. In the 2013 White House Initiative on HBCUs, it was reported that the Department of Education was the major provider of financial aid to HBCU students. In a discussion paper written by John Michael Lee, Jr. and Samaad Wes Keys, they report in 2011 the percentage of students receiving Pell Grants was 49 percent at all institutions (p.15). However, at HBCUs the recipients were a great deal higher at 71 percent (Lee & Keys, 2013). Financial aid is what allows HBCU students to attend college and for some tuition-dependent institutions it allows them to keep the doors open and the heat on.

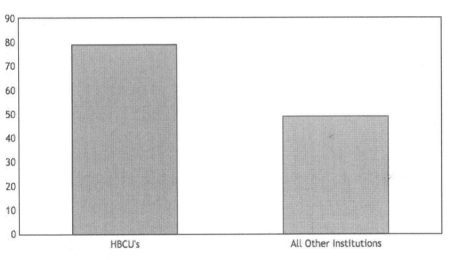

2011 Pell Grant Distributions (in Percent)

Financial Aid

More than half of undergraduates in this country get some form of financial aid. Financial aid can include grants, scholarships, work study, and student and parent loans. Financial aid is provided to students and families in need (Wilkerson, 2005). Student and parent loans are very different from grants and scholarships and must be paid back with interest. Federal loan programs are included in federal financial aid because they offer loans below market rates (Carey, 2013).

They also provide access to credit that would not be available to some families. Unfortunately grants provided to students for college and family incomes have not kept pace with the escalation of costs at four-year colleges and universities. For lower income families, financial aid and loans make up a majority of their university resources. For many African American families HBCUs appear to be the best option when hoping to realize the college dream. Even for families who planned for college, the recent economic crisis that caused the unemployment rate to rise can be a challenge for middle class families as college tuition continued to rise despite the economic climate. HBCUs have remained lower in costs than other institutions around the country (Wilkerson, 2005). Students also gain a small private education experience at a cost that is considerably less than what is found at comparable non-HBCUs (Richards, 2015).

The United Negro College Fund reports in its updated study: Affordability of UNFC-Member Institutions, HBCUs continue to be affordable. The report compared the costs of the 37 HBCU's that comprise the UNCF network to other comparable private- not-for-profit institutions around the country. The UNCF study found that during the 2007 recession to the present, despite tuition increases around the country, the cost to attend the 37 HBCUs were significantly lower than the comparison institutions. The average total tuition of the UNCF members in the 2012-13 academic years was $26,433. UNCF members were $9,353 lower than the compared institutions in the same year (Richards, 2014, p.11).

Although HBCUs are affordable compared to other schools, students who attend HBCU's still depend greatly on financial aid. The National Center of Education Statistics reported the ercentage of undergraduate students' federal, state and local institutional or other sources of aid from 2009 to 2012. It found the average range from 81% to 87% in 2012.[2]

Pell Grant

The Federal Pell Grant program and the Parent PLUS loan programs are of issue here. The Pell Grant program is the single largest source of federal aid supporting postsecondary education. According to the Congressional Research Service in the Federal Pell Grant Program of Higher Education Act Report, Pell Grants are need-based aid intended to be the foundation for all student aid awarded to undergraduates. The federal government states there is no absolute income threshold that determines who is eligible. All in all, 63% of dependent and 84% of independent Pell grant recipients in 2009, had total family incomes at or below $30,000.[3]

In 2011, the federal government limited the ability of students to use Pell Grants from 18 semesters to 12 semesters. The federal government also ended summer Pell Grants which has also had an impact on the HBCU community (Lee & Keys, 2013). According to an article from Inside Higher Education, by Ry Rivard (2014), of the 85 percent of students who attend HBCUs and receive Pell Grants, only one third take less than six years to graduate. The HBCUs lose tuition revenues because students cannot afford to keep attending. Many HBCU's have fewer resources than predominately White institutions and are trying to educate students with less college preparation. It appears now that HBCUs are getting punished for not getting swift and extraordinary results (Rivard, 2014). This will affect an HBCU's tuition revenue.

---

[2] National Center of Education Statistics. 2012. "HBCU Financial Aid" IPEDS. 2009-2012.
[3] Mahan, S.M. (2011, May 12) Federal Pell Grant Program of the Higher Education Act: Recent Changes, and Current Legislative Issues. *Congressional Research Service*. p.19

The Pell Grant is not the only issue HBCUs are nervous about. High default rates can cause institutions to face sanctions and possible loss of accreditation.

Cohort Default Rate

HBCUs have had exemptions to financial aid defaults throughout the 1990's. Default for an institution occurs when a school that has more than 30 or more borrowers entering repayment in the fiscal year, the schools' default rate is a percentage of the schools' borrowers that enter repayment. If more than 30 percent of those borrowers in the federal loan programs, Federal Family Education Loans (FFELS) or William D. Ford Federal Direct Loans (Direct Loans) are in default, then the school can be sanctioned.

For students, default means not making payments according to the scheduled payments agreed to in their contract/promissory note. The federal government considers a loan in default when borrower payments are monthly and the borrower fails to pay for 270 days. When a borrowers payments are less than once a month default occurs when a borrower fails to make a payment in 330 days. It also may mean their taxes could be withheld, wages may be garnished and may cause serious consequences to their school.[4] These recent changes to the Higher Education Act are cause for great concern for HBCUs. HBCUs serve a large population of at-risk students. Incurring default penalties would mean any HBCUs would become ineligible to participate in federal student loan programs. HBCUs and tribally controlled colleges were exempt from the default threshold in the past (Devarics, 1998, p.8).

Section 435(a)(2) of the Higher Education Act of 1965, as amended, provides that institutions lose eligibility to participate in the Federal Direct Loan and Federal Pell Grant programs when

---

[4] Department of Education. Understanding Default: Don't ignore your student loan payments or you'll risking going into default. https://studentaid.ed.gov/repay-loans/default

the institutions' federal student loan Cohort Default Rate (CDR) exceeds 30 percent for each of the three most recently completed federal fiscal years beginning with federal fiscal year 2012.[5] The intent of the change was to give a clearer indication of whether institutions and lenders are educating students on to how to repay their loans and to also keep track of how much student loan debt is accrued by students. HBCUs already assist many students who come from academically deficient high schools and require more resources when they enter college. The changes to the Pell Grant and other financial assistance provided by the federal government may cause an increasing number of minority students to drop out as they reach the Pell Grant 12-semester limit. If students are unable to finish their college education in time, they cannot get a college degree without other investment resources. Without a degree they are unlikely to land jobs or pursue careers that lead to competitive living wages. This creates a problem for HBCUs when an institutional default rate exceeds 30 percent (Rivard, 2014). Institutions need to know how the process works. There are choices available to schools in trouble. Institutions have the opportunity to appeal once notified that their official default rate percentage will produce a school sanction. Understanding the cohort default rate can be difficult. We will make an attempt to explain how the cohort default rate works and how institutions appeal.

When an institution's three most recent official cohort default rates are 30 percent or greater for the three-year calculation, the institution may be sanctioned. Without a successful adjustment or appeal, the institution will lose their Direct Loan and Federal Pell Grant program

---

[5] Department of Education, Federal Student Aid Portfolio Performance Division, (2014) Fact Sheet Historical Black Colleges, 12-1 FY 2011 3-Year Cohort Default Rates September. http://www2.ed.gov/offices/OSFAP/defaultmanagement/dmd002.html

eligibility for the rest of the fiscal year in which the school was notified and for the following two fiscal years. [6]

If a school is notified that they are subject to sanctions, the school may submit an appeal within 30 days of receiving notice in order to avoid the sanctions. Some of the ways to challenge sanctions include: A Thirty-or Fewer Borrowers Appeal occurs when an institution can demonstrate a low borrower participation rate to avoid an anticipated sanction (p. 2.4-5). Meaning the school can show in the sequence of three years there were less than 30 borrowers. For example: this year four borrowers, last year, there were six borrowers and two years ago there were seven borrowers. In those three years there were only 17 borrowers. With fewer than thirty borrowers the appeal will be successful and the school will not be sanctioned.[7]

---

[6] Department of Education. Federal Student Aid Cohort Default Rate Effects.(Sanctions and Benefits). Retrieved from http://ifap.ed.gov/DefaultManagement/guide/attachments/CDRMasterFile.pdf p. 2.4-4
[7] Department of Education. Federal Student Aid Cohort Default Rate Effects.(Thirty-or-Fewer Borrowers Appeal: Low Borrowers). Retrieved from
http://ifap.ed.gov/DefaultManagement/guide/attachments/CDRGuideCh4Pt1030orfewer.pdf p. 4.1- 2

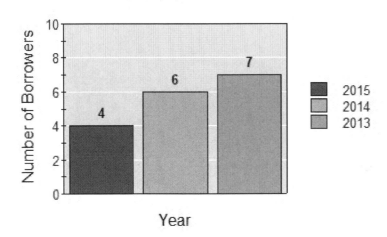

Borrowers

The Economically Disadvantaged Appeal, is used when an institution can demonstrate one of two types of appeals. (1) Economically disadvantaged based on low income. (2) Low completion rate. The appeals process varies upon whether it is a degree-granting institution. For the purpose of this text, we will examine only the degree-granting institution appeal.[8] Only a degree granting institution can submit an appeal for low income and low completion rate (p.4.7-8).

The low income appeal requires the school to show two-thirds or more of the percentage of the students are low income. The percentage is determined during a 12-month period within the three-year cohort. The school may select the 12-month period that most benefits the institution (p.4.7-3). Within the selected 12-month period the school calculates the students eligible for the

[8] Department of Education. Federal Student Aid Cohort Default Rate Effects. (Economically Disadvantaged Appeal: Low Income Students). Retrieved from http://ifap.ed.gov/DefaultManagement/guide/attachments/CDRGuideCh4Pt7EDA.pdf p. 4.7-2

loan program (FFEL) that have been enrolled at least half time and have attended at least one day during the 12-month period.

The school determines low income using one of two methods: (a) examining the Expected Family Contribution (EFC) and (b) analyzing the Adjusted Gross income (AGI) of a student or family.

(A) If the Expected Family Contribution (EFC) is equal or less than EFC required to allow a student to receive half of the maximum Pell Grant, the student is low income. Meaning regardless of students enrollment status or cost, if the student EFC qualifies them for half of the maximum award, they are considered low income and can be included in the percentage of students for the appeal (p. 4.7-5).

(B) The other way a degree granting institution determines who are low income students, is by computing the student Adjusted Gross Income (AGI). If the student's parents' or spouses' contribution (independent student) is less than the Department of Health and Human Services poverty guidelines for the student's family unit. If the students fit the low income criteria they may be included in the 12-month period calculation. To determine the low income rate, a school must divide the number of low income students that fit the criteria above by the total number of students in an eligible loan program (p. 4.7-5).

(2) The other economically disadvantage appeal involves the low completion rate challenge. When calculating the completion rate a school must again use the 12-month period. The schedule is determined by the school's enrollment contract or catalog (p. 4.7-8).

Those scheduled to complete students are divided by those students who have completed their program. A student is considered completed if the meet one of the following criteria: (a) the student completed the educational program in which they were enrolled. (b) The student transferred to a higher level program at another school. (c) The student remained enrolled and was making satisfactory academic progress at the end of the 12-month period. (d) The student entered active duty in the U.S. Armed Forces (p. 4.7-8).

$$\left| \frac{Completed\ Students}{Scheduled\ to\ Complete} \right. = \text{A Completion Rate}$$

Even if the challenges above are successful; it does not change the schools cohort default rate. It only allows the institution an exemption from loss of eligibility to disburse loans, until the next official cohort default rate calculation.

The appeals process gives institutions an opportunity to push back and explain the high default rates. For HBCUs with the economy in recession and the resulting lack of jobs, repaying student loans may not be possible. Walter M. Kimborough, President of Dillard University in New Orleans stated in an article for the Tampa Bay Times:" The major issue is HBCUs serve a population that has little wealth, lower incomes and higher unemployment. When this is the community you serve, you are going to have financial issues (Maxwell, 2013).

Parent PLUS Loans

In addition to Pell Grants the federal government has also changed eligibility requirements for Parent PLUS Loans. According to Julianne Malveaux 's article in USA Today (2013), the federal government changed its credit rating standing which has led to a drop in approval ratings for parents from 45% before the change in the 2011-12 academic year to 24% in 2012-13. Some parents feel the changes are an attack on HBCUs. Malveaux, who attended an HBCU, states the federal government's changes in the Pell Grant and Parent PLUS Loan programs left 28,000 HBCU students stranded in the fall of 2012 (Malveaux, 2013).

The amount a student can borrow is capped between $5,500 and $7, 500 per year in Federal Stafford loans. Parents with the Parent PLUS loan on the other hand, can borrow the full price of attendance (Nelson, 2012). The cost of attendance is determined by the institution and may include room, board, and living expenses along with tuition and fees. At more expensive colleges, costs may reach $50,000 a year (Carey, 2013).

The 2011 Pell Grant change from 18 to 12 semesters, also included the Parent PLUS loans (Field, 2013). The Parent PLUS Loan change involved a closer look at the borrower's credit history. An applicant can be rejected for an adverse credit history -- an account in collection or a recent charge off as unpayable in the last five years (Stafford, 2014). Many argue this change, which occurred without so much as an explanation, has caused loan denial to reach 50% (Field, 2013). A coalition representing HBCUs and members of the Congressional Black Caucus were prepared to sue. The group wrote the National Association for Equal Opportunity of Higher Education. The response of the education department was a promise to revisit the issue (Field, 2013). The education department has been under intense pressure and has promised to reconsider lowering the standards.

In the past, borrowers were rejected for having an account in collection for more than 90 days (Stafford, 2014). Basically any parent could apply as long as they had a decent credit history. The default rates of Parent PLUS loans are lower than other federal loans. However, because Parent PLUS loans are subject to some credit-screening, it may be the reason the Parent PLUS loan borrowers perform better compared to other federal college loan programs. The other loan programs are open to everyone regardless of credit history (Stafford, 2014). The Parent PLUS delinquent borrowers have the right to appeal, but HBCU presidents say appeals are insufficient.

Without Parent PLUS loans, enrollment has dropped for several HBCUs. As of June 2013, in an article by Kevin Carey (2013) in the Chronicle of Higher Education, it was reported that Morehouse was forced to furlough many faculty and staff members. Between fall of 2011 and spring of 2013, Clark Atlanta University saw its loan denial rate increase from 25 percent to 65 percent and saw an enrollment drop of 334 students. Howard University has seen a loan denial of 607 and Florida A&M University a denial of 569 (Carey, 2013). Morgan State held an emergency fundraising drive with hope of raising $300,000 for 300 students whose parents were denied the Parent PLUS Loan (Doubleday, 2013). However, Morgan was only able to raise 100,000 for 100 student scholarships, but school officials remained positive and stated that is a 100 students we do not have to send home (Doubleday, 2013). The impact does not stop there. According to the Association of Public and Land-Grant Universities (APLU) Fact Sheet: The five schools which saw the most denied loans in the Fall of 2012 were (1) North Carolina Central University (NC) 609 denials, (2) Howard University (DC) 607 denials, (3) Florida A&M University (FL) 569 loan rejections, (4) Prairie View A &M (TX) had 528 parent loans turned away, and (5) Grambling State University (LA) had 523 parents denied the PLUS loan (Lee and Keys, 2013,p. 1).[9] These are devastating numbers for HBCUs. The Thurgood Marshal College Fund has threatened to sue the federal government over the changes in the Parent PLUS Loans (Carey, 2013).

Controversy

Consumer advocates believe the changes should not be reversed. To return to the screening methods of the past would cause families to go further into debt and take out loans they cannot possibly repay. The loans are brokered at an interest rate of seven to nine percent and unlike student loans, they cannot be deferred after graduation (Carey, 2013). In addition, Parent PLUS Loans are not easy to discharge in bankruptcy. The loan does not qualify for income-based

Lee, J.M. and Keys, S.W. (2013). *Impact of Parent PLUS Loan Changes on Historically Black Colleges and Universities*. (APLU Office of Access and Success publication no. 3000-FS1). Washington, DC: Association of Public and Land-grant Universities.

repayment unlike other federal college loans which can limit loan payments to 10 percent of income and forgives the remaining debt after 20 years (Carey, 2013). Furthermore, the Parent PLUS loan debt may put retirement accounts and Social Security benefits at risk of garnishment (Carey, 2013).

Colleges do not receive sanctions or punishment for large numbers of PLUS Loan borrowers. The Department of Education does not tally college level default rates for PLUS Loans. The department only releases data for for-profit institutions, private, non-profit and public institutions, but no individual institutional level information (Stratford, 2013).

HBCUs Fight Back

A financial crisis can cause an institution to lose accreditation. In order to avoid this financial crisis and shutting doors, HBCUs had no choice but to fight the changes to the Pell grant and the Parent PLUS loans. On September 6, 2012, the Presidents Board of Advisors on HBCUs, UNCF and The National Association for Equal Opportunity in Higher Education wrote a letter to U.S. Department of Education Secretary Arne Duncan.[10] The letter was spearheaded by Hampton University President William Harvey with Negro College Fund President and CEO Michael Lomax. In it; they expressed concern that the changes to Parent PLUS loans were having an impact on their institutions and students. The letter asked for a fair and reasonable interpretation of the credit history requirement (UNFC, 2014, p.9). The written request asked for better interpretation of appeals processes with use of "extenuating circumstances "provision of the

---

[10] UNF Fredrick D. Patterson Research Institute. (2014). The Parent PLUS Loan Crisis: An Urgent Crisis Facing Students at the Nation's HBCUs. UNCF.org Washington, DC.

regulations (UNFC, 2014). The HBCU community also asked for grandfathering in students who applied for loans prior to 2012 (UNFC, 2014).

The letter opened the door to a meeting between HBCU leaders and Secretary Arne Duncan (UNFC, 2014, p.10). The Secretary agreed to initiate an appeals process and would provide a toll free number for parents to use who have been denied contact with the Department of education. However, the secretary refused to drop the new credit standards or to reverse the denials. In November 2012, the Department of Education pledges to consider parents of students who had received Parent PLUS loans in the past under the Department's "extenuating circumstances authority" (UNFC, 2014, p.16).

In June of 2013 Seventeen HBCU presidents and senior officials and students gathered at Spellman College to impress upon Department of Education officials the negative impact the restrictive Parent PLUS standards have on college accessibility (UNFC, 2014, p.17). In August 2013, Secretary Duncan writes a letter to U.S. Representative Marcia Fudge, the Congressional Black Caucus Chairperson, stating there will be a loosening of Parent PLUS Loan standards, but delays actual rulemaking until spring 2014 (UNFC, 2014). Representative Fudge, a Democrat from Ohio rejects the proposal and demands a real solution to the problem. Fudge, demanded the Department suspend the new Parent PLUS policy completely and immediately.[11]

At the National Historically Black College and Universities conference on September 22, 2014, Dr. William R. Harvey, President of Hampton University, in his opening remarks stated that Washington needs to know we are watching and we are counting (Morris, 2014). In the

---

[1] Marybeth Gasman & Heather Collins (2014) The Historically Black College and University Community and the Obama Administration: A Lesson in Communication, Change: The Magazine of Higher Learning, 46:5, 39-43, DOI:
0.1080/00091383.2014.941770

article: HBCUs on Edge, in the Chronicle of the Higher Education, President Harvey went on to say the Parent PLUS loan situation has been a debacle. His statements opened a flurry of critique on the Department of Education, during the conference, representatives from the department participated in a panel discussion (Morris, 2014). The Department of Education defended their decisions and admitted their errors. They offered apologies for the flaws in the changes in the PLUS loan. Representatives said they will be reconsidering the current changes in 2014.

In February of 2014, the education department convened a rulemaking committee to consider the definition of "adverse credit history" under the Parent PLUS Loan program and names Dr. David Swinton, president of Benedict College, and Dr. George French, president of Miles College as negotiators for minority serving organizations (UNFC, 2014, p. 18). The HBCU community definitely has the ear of Secretary Duncan, the hope is their demands will be met. The hope is the new changes will cease. The HBCU community has taken action now they wait for change.

A Sigh of Relief

The Department of Education offers relief for many community colleges and HBCUs. The department decided to make an adjustment in their calculations of the default rate. On September 23, 2014, Jeff Baker, Director, Policy Liaison and Implementation of Federal Student Aid, announced in a memorandum there would be an adjustment in the Cohort Default Rate (Baker, 2014). [12] With the recent changes to the Federal Student Loan Programs, the Education

[12] Baker, J. (2014, September 23). Adjustment of Calculation of Official Three Year Cohort Default Rates for Institutions Subject to Potential Loss of Eligibility. *Information for Financial Aid Professional- Department of education*. (Electronic announcement) retrieved from http://www.ifap.ed.gov/eannouncements/092314AdjustmentofCalculationofOfc3YrCDRforInsti tutSubtoPotentialLossofElig.html

Department had to take under consideration the many borrowers in the cohort who have more than one federal student loan. Although new rules require loans to be serviced by Direct Loans, many in the cohort are still being administered by the Federal Family Education Loan program (Baker, 2014).

In calculating default rates, the department looks at a cohort of loan borrowers at an institution and then tallies how many borrowers have defaulted on loans three years after entering repayment (Stratford & Fain, 2014). The education department looked at the schools on the verge of losing federal aid, and provided an adjustment in their calculation. If the borrower had more than one loan and one of the loans was not in default then it negated the defaulted loans. Then they were removed from the default count. The non-default loan had to be in repayment, deferment or forbearance for at least 60 days to be removed from the tally (Stratford & Fain, 2014).

The Department of Education took into consideration the split service with which many borrowers deal. Split services are when a borrower's student loan debt is managed by different companies. Split services occurred when the department began buying some loans issued through now-defunct federal bank-based loans. It can be difficult to keep track of your loans if they are not consolidated or not managed by one company. So, if one loan is in non-default it can remove the borrower from the calculation giving the institution a lower default rate (Stratford, 2014).

The adjustment was applied retroactively to colleges' three year default rate. The penalties apply when the default rate reaches the levels set by Congress. When a college's default rate is

30 percent or higher for three consecutive years or if an institutions default rate sky rockets to 40 percent in any single year (Baker, 2014).

Without the calculation change, there would have been major sanctions for HBCUs. There were 14 HBCUs that had default rates above 30 percent in the 2011 three-year cohort (Baker, 2014). This was a great relief for institutions that feared a loss in financial aid and accreditation. However, some colleges and universities remain in jeopardy. The adjustment in the calculations of default borrowers is only temporary. Despite the push from HBCU presidents and student advocates, the Department of Education has not decided if the adjustment will continue (Stratford, 2014). This respite may provide institutions with an opportunity to close ranks and lower their default rate before the sanctions kick back in.

According to a fact sheet released by the Department of Education, as of September 2014, all 101 eligible HBCUs have official FY 2011 three-year Cohort Default Rates that fall below regulatory thresholds. No HBCUs are subject to CDR sanctions or the consequent loss of Direct Loan and Pell Grant student financial assistance program eligibility.[13] According to the Department's fact sheet, it is not the CDR calculation adjustment that has helped HBCUs, it is the programs and changes the institutions have initiated.

As stated in the department's September 2014 fact sheet, HBCUs have enacted strategies that include implementation of a default management plan that engages stakeholders, identifies approaches to reducing default rates, and tracks measurable goals.[14] HBCUs have increased

---

[13] Department of Education, Federal Student Aid Portfolio Performance Division, (2014) Fact Sheet Historical Black Colleges, 12-1 FY 2011 3-Year Cohort Default Rates September. http://www2.ed.gov/offices/OSFAP/defaultmanagement/dmd002.html

[14] Department of Education, Federal Student Aid Portfolio Performance Division, (2014) Fact

borrower awareness of obligations through incorporating borrower topics at orientation sessions and providing enhanced entrance and exit counseling.[15]

The Controversy

There is some question as to whether the Department of Education has the statutory power to change the way default rates are calculated. Furthermore, should cohort default relief only apply to those schools in trouble (Stratford & Fain, 2014)? Should it be just the same for everyone? Many of the articles discussing the matter fear such measures may be legally arbitrary. By making changes and offering reliefs for institutions in distress there arises a concern that schools will not be held accountable for defaults. The department gives a reprieve to institutions, but the student does not get one. The student will still owe on the loan even though they are not counted in the institution's default (Stratford &Fain).

Winning

In October 22, 2014, the Department of Education announced a final rule to Federal PLUS Loans.[16] To make sure families are able to pay for college. The government hopes the changes

---

Sheet Historical Black Colleges, 12-1 FY 2011 3-Year Cohort Default Rates September. http://www2.ed.gov/offices/OSFAP/defaultmanagement/dmd002.html

[5] Department of Education, Federal Student Aid Portfolio Performance Division, (2014) Fact Sheet Historical Black Colleges, 12-1 FY 2011 3-Year Cohort Default Rates September. http://www2.ed.gov/offices/OSFAP/defaultmanagement/dmd002.html

[6] Department of Education White House Initiative on Historically Black College and Universities.2014. " US Department of Education Announces Final Rule to Strengthens Federal Direct PLUS Loan Program.pg.1

will expand access to a college education, safeguard taxpayer dollars and reflect current economic changes.

U.S. Secretary of Education Arne Duncan updated the borrower's standards. The Department is developing a new loan counseling tool that would provide customized information to assist PLUS borrowers (White House, 2014, p.2). There will be clearer definitions. The new rule will define "charge off" and "in collection" for borrowers to better understand if they have an adverse credit history (White House, 2014, p .3).

Some of the changes include establishing a debt threshold of $2,085 that are 90 or more days delinquent as of the date of the credit report to fit current inflation rates (White House, 2014). Anything below this threshold amount a borrower is not considered to have an adverse credit history. The other changes include reducing time periods of the borrower's considered credit history. It has been reduced from five years to two years (White House, 2014). Furthermore, if a borrower does have an adverse credit history, they may still be able to get a PLUS loan if they are able to demonstrate extenuating circumstances, obtain an endorser or participate in loan counseling (White House, 2014).

This final rule reflects extensive research and outreach by the Department of Education. The department held four hearings around the country in Washington, DC. Minneapolis, Minnesota, San Francisco, California and Atlanta, Georgia, and collected recommendations and feedback from students, parents, institutions and community organizations.[17] If parties were unable to

[17]Office of the Federal Register, (2014, August 8). William D. Ford Direct Loan Program: Notice of proposed rulemaking press release. Press Media Solutions.

attend the hearings, they were invited to submit comments in writing (Federal Register, 2014, p.6). HBCUs win in this outcome. The new rule will hopefully allow those denied parents the ability to assist their children with a college education. The goal of the loan programs were to provide access to education. Let's hope the doors remain at Historical Black Colleges and Universities. Because Blacks and other minority students deserve the opportunity no matter the cost.

Chapter 13

Poor Customer Service - the Reason Some HBCUs Are Destined To Fail

Dr. T. Andrus

Customer service is without a doubt the most important factor when determining whether a college will succeed or fail. Many researchers may disagree with me on this point and focus on other factors such as revenue, infrastructure, athletics, academics and the such but in reality none of these would be possible with continued poor customer service. Customer service is the key to long-term sustainability of colleges and universities whether HBCUs or PWIs. Customer service is the lifeblood of all colleges and universities. When great customer service is offered to students, faculty and staff everyone involved are happier, relaxed and enjoy a greater sense of pride and belonging to the institutions.

Historically Black Colleges and Universities are in a very unique position to offer services to the masses of students matriculating out of high school, military and those who are displaced from their jobs for whatever reasons. Many students seeking admission into colleges and universities want to attend institutions that are well organized, has great academic programs to offer, welcome diversity and has various extracurricular sports and activities to offer the students. Paramount to the aforementioned is customer service. Students expect colleges to be more organized than their high schools that they just graduated from and for these students to come to an institution of higher education and find services in a disarray is unacceptable! Students expect more and will not settle for less when it comes to their education and customer service.

Customer service is the provision of **service** to **customers** before, during and after a purchase. Accordingly, it may vary by product, **service**, industry and individual **customer**. The perception of success of such interactions is dependent on employees "who can adjust themselves to the personality of the guest".

In our particular case the students are our guest. Can we adjust ourselves to the personality of our guest? We want to put our best feet forward from day one. Customer service should be offered from the onset of recruiting to the first day of class. Admissions should be in constant contact with potential applicants and should establish open lines of communications with all of these students. Students should be constantly updated on their admission status. The mere fact that a college or university will forward correspondence to a student speaks volumes for the institution where students are concerned. Students love receiving mail from colleges and universities trying to recruit them to their institutions. Potential students should be contacted and updated on their housing status. Students should not have to come to school guessing where they will be housed. Students should receive their credentialing information prior to ever arriving at their college or university. Preferably, students should be able to attend Visit-Us or pre-enrollment registration symposiums so that they can complete all necessary paperwork and get their schedules prior to arriving on campus.

Once students arrive on campus they should be greeted by upperclassmen who help to guide them in their first weeks of class. Students should be given opportunities to ask questions and share their concerns with the administration as well as their peers. Students should be aware of what they can and cannot bring to their chosen institutions. Students should be able to be served in centralized locations for concerns with admissions, financial aid, registrar etc. Students should never have to walk across campus over and over again because faculty and staff members are not sure about who can help our students. Good customer service would dictate that the faculty or staff member pick up the phone and gather the needed information for the students to help avoid them becoming frustrated and discouraged. No one wants to get the run-arounds when they are trying to take care of business. We need to be able to send students directly to those who are able to help them.

Faculty must be ready to teach on the first day of class! No students should have to attend the first day of class and find an empty class room. The faculty's job is to meet, greet and teach students from day one. The first day of class actually set the tone for the rest of the semester. When faculty members are not present, not organized nor prepared for the first day of class, they send a message to the student that not being prepared is ok. While faculty have academic freedom and are able to use their discretion, faculty must never abuse their rights to modify their syllabi and schedules to accommodate their personal agendas. Colleges and universities should be ready on day one with room assignments. All courses should have assigned classrooms from day one. Faculty and students should not be forced to find classrooms to meet in because of a mix-up in classroom assignments. Logistics is key here. Schools must be pro-active in regards to how classroom space will be used. Administrators must ensure that all classes are not being offered on Monday, Wednesday and Friday from 10-2 or on Tuesday and Thursday from 9-1. The classroom space is not the problem in most cases, the times that the courses are offered are usually the problem. Faculty nor most students want to go to class at 8AM or after 3PM. Good customer services will dictate that classes be taught from 8AM to 5PM for traditional students and from 6PM to 10PM for non-traditional students.

Students should be advised properly from day one. No students should end their first semester in college without a signed degree plan that will outline the courses that they will need to satisfy their degree requirements. That degree plan should be signed by their advisor. Advisors should be available to assist their advisee during their office hours. Good customer service means

138

having an open door policy for students. Students perform better academically and continue to matriculate at a much higher rate when they are able to stay closely connected to their advisors and faculty.

Student should be encouraged to seek internships and they should be advises of the potential setbacks they might encounter with low GPAs. Students should be advised of the perils of have criminal backgrounds and the impact their choices will have on their chances of future employment. Even misdemeanor charges can greatly hamper their chances of landing their dream job. They should know from day one that there are consequences for criminal activity.

Great customer service should extend way beyond the student's graduation. Colleges and universities are now required by the government to track their graduates. Colleges and departments should be able to track their graduates for five to seven years after graduation to see how well prepared they were for their jobs. Students should be interviewed and forwarded copies of their department newsletters so that they can stay abreast of happening at their alma maters. Students who leave colleges and universities on a good note are much more inclined to contribute financially to their alma-maters.

Chapter 14

Characteristics That Will Ensure the Survival of HBCUs

Dr. T. Andrus

Historically Black Colleges and Universities are the lifeblood of black America. America and African Americans need HBCUs. There is no experience like the HBCU experience for African Americans. As we enter into 2016 we must become more vigilant and focused on how we can better serve our students at HBCUs. African American students are the lifeblood of HBCUs. Many faculty and staff members at HWCUs are not willing to take the time, effort and patience to work with our students as much as we are. With our students comes opportunities for diverse learning. We must adjust our teaching styles to try and reach all students in our class rooms. HBCUs must improve services to our clients the African American students if we are to stay relevant in the future. We cannot take the students for granted. We need them and they need us. When we improve in these areas: Cafeteria, transparency, dorms-parents, failure to return calls, answer phones, reply in a timely manner, losing documents, disconnect in language barriers, graduation audits, degree plans, grades, poor record keeping, carelessness, professors are no shows – late, not prepared, disorganization of classrooms on the first day of school, server is down and cannot access online classes, professors who refuse to work with students, failure to give students their refund in a timely manner.

HBCUs seem to focus more on non-academic scholarships than academics yet we say that our focus is on education. While we realize that sports and extracurricular activities are vital to most institutions it is imperative that we focus on the academic success of our students. We must offer more academic scholarships to our students and use these scholarships as recruiting tools for our schools even if the scholarships are partial. Scholarships should be used as incentives for attracting students.

If a student has a tuition of $4000.00 per semester and he or she is given a $1500.00 scholarship and a Pell grant pays the remaining $2500.00 for the student that would amount to a full ride scholarship. If this student is a cream of the crop/high achieving student we can use creative financing/scholarships to attract these students to our institutions. Attracting the cream of the crop students has a recurring effect on the student population in which that student comes from.

In order to serve our students more efficiently we must find out what they want and how we can make their stay at the college better. I believe that the greatest predictor of satisfaction for students at any college or university is customer satisfaction. If students are not satisfied with the customer service at any college or university that will result in a bad experience which results in negative publicity. If the students are not happy their experiences will be unpleasant and their experiences will result in bad publicity for the colleges and universities that they attend. Real life advertising whether negative or positive have a significant impact on the hearer and in many cases will form permanent opinions in the mind of the hearer that can cause them to make final decisions as to whether they will attend or not attend a college or university. No college or university is an island and no college or university stands alone! All colleges and universities need students and need to treat the students like they are needed. When colleges and universities lose their zeal to offer superb customer service they begin their demise because customer service is the lifeblood of any organization. Give the HBCU students more options in the cafeteria and in the area of entertainment, extracurricular activities and academic exercises.

African American Students as a result of receiving great customer services will feel obligated to give back to their institutions. HBCUs must offer superb customer services to their students throughout their matriculation. Department and divisions with excellent customer service usually see increases in their enrollment, have higher graduation rates and retention rates etc. HBCUs can significantly increase their endowments if they concentrate more on customer service, feature more groups of students in their magazines, highlight monthly alumni that are making a difference and impacting their fields, send alumni a pencil, pad or memorabilia from the college or university so that they can take pride in their alma maters. People like attention whether we want to admit it or not, therefore HBCUs must provide specific events to attract specific groups and classes to annual events hosted by the colleges and universities. Another way to increase endowments would be through financial campaigns sponsored through Greek organizations. Greek organizations give money annually to renew their dues. Greeks would gladly give $120.00 or more a year to their alma maters if they felt a strong connection to the colleges and universities that they pledged at. Finally HBCUs must be more vigilant in their pursuit to court fortune 500 corporations, millionaires and billionaires. We must see ourselves as being worthy enough to approach billionaire philanthropist to see generous financial gifts and most of all we must have an executable plan drafted on how the funds will be spend. Many organizations and philanthropists would be willing to give if HBCUs have well documented plans and narratives in place to explain how the collected funds will be spent. HBCUs need more unrestricted funds so that they can be more innovative in their approach to offer cutting edge global education to their students. All HBCUs should have STEM labs in place that could be used by interdisciplinary programs.

HBCUs must aggressively seek out contributions from Fortune Five hundred corporations and successful enterprises in America and abroad. African Americans and HBCU employees and students are responsible for keeping many businesses and corporations in business because of our patronizing of their businesses. While we understand that corporations donate billions of dollars each year and that they cannot give to all entities, we equally understand that portions of their donations can be shared with HBCUs. The United Negro College Fund is already in a great position to request, receive and disburse these funds to all HBCUs. We can no longer retain the attitude that HBCUs cannot approach certain donors of certain corporations because they are not alumni of our colleges and universities. We must seek donations based upon our patronizing and our future commitments to purchase products. The world is now flat! We know whose purchasing products and services. We know who is patronizing businesses with the click of the mouse. African Americans are primarily consumers and therefore continues to spend billions of dollars on products and services every year. Now is the time to ask for returns on our investments. AT&T, Verizon, Sprint, Ford, GM, Chrysler, GE, Coke, Microsoft, Dell, Timex, Nike, Hershey, Time Warner, Shell, Chevron, Exxon-Mobil, Pharmaceutical Companies, Food Manufacturers etc. should be courted for millions of dollars annually to support HBCU's. The success of students graduating from HBCUs will continue to make it possible for these graduates to have the spending power to patronize these businesses.

Chapter 15

A Brief Glimpse of the Future Sustainability of Historically Black Colleges and Universities

Dr. Tracy Andrus

Historically Black Colleges and Universities were formed to educate newly freed slaves so that they would be able to educate other slaves and their children. The main purpose for the establishment of HB CUs were to make sure that there were separate but equal institutions of higher learning for African Americans after reconstruction. Under the Morrill Act HBCUs thrived during the turn of the 20th century. During the four decades between 1880 and 1920 many HBCUs were formed and are still thriving today.

HBCUs have proved to be the backbone and preserver of African American Culture and has continued unto this day to educate more African Americans than any other institutions in America. According to HBCU connect (2015) African Americans who graduate from HBCUs have continued to thrive much better than those who have graduated from Predominately White Institutions (PWIs).

Today HBCUs are continuing to thrive but there is trouble on the horizon. Big government, competition, limited financial aid, reductions in parent plus loans, reduced cost and free tuition at community colleges, open admissions at community colleges among other things have resulted in a decrease in enrollment at HBCUs. While African American students are graduating at the highest levels in history, the sustainability of HBCUs continue to be threatened by the powers that be, big government and those who think that HBCUs have finished their course and should be integrated with large public and private institutional systems. PWI institutions and others continue to offer HBCUs an opportunity to join their systems through methodical methods of integration. What they don't tell these institutions is that once they sign on the dotted line they will no longer have control of their institutions. Yes, they will support the institutors financially but in reality these institutions would have signed their deeds over to the PWIs and now they along with their monies will control our institutions. Can HBCUs afford to turn over our institutions to PWIs? I think not! We must at all cost remain independent! Our student have special needs and we are the only ones that will provide the services and educational support for our people. While this may sound harsh we all know that this is the true! We cannot chance the education of our youth to anyone other than HBCUs. That is why I urge all fraternities, government officials, educators, CEOs, and citizens to support the United Negro College Fund (UNCF) and organizations that support Black Higher Education. A mind is a terrible thing to waste!

In recent years several HBCUs have had to close their doors for various reasons which have included among other things financial exigencies, academic problems and failure to submit requested documents in a timely manner. African Americans cannot afford to allow any other HBCU institutions to close their doors. If we all work together we can make sure that no other HBCU is forced to close their doors. I love HBCUs and I am a product of an HBCU Prairie View A&M University in Prairie View, Texas.

I wrote this book to remind HBCUs that customer service is very important in any industry but especially in higher education. HBCUs must make sure that they are offering the best customer services to all of our students.

Black Students at Predominantly White Colleges

Finally, it is important to note that as I complete this book black students at Mizzou are still protesting and the President of the Missouri campus Tim Wolfe has just tendered his resignation effective immediately. Black students are protesting the handling of racial discrimination complaints by the Missouri campus. This protest has led to additional protest at other colleges and universities such as the University of California, Irvine, Ithaca University in New York, Smith College, Yale, and Claremont Colleges to name a few.

Students are becoming more concerned about the insensitivity of college administrators regarding the treatment of concerns reported by minorities on predominantly white campuses. I thank God today for social media and the cell phone. With my cell phone and social media I am my own news station. I don't have to wait for CNN, FOX or ABC to broadcast news in my community, at my college or at the local park, We now have the power to make known what is important to us. As we move closer to 2016 we will discover more acts of racism, corruption, insensitivity and underlining biases at many colleges and universities. I believe that all colleges and universities black or white have underlining motives that are somewhat ulterior.

But the question of the 21st century in regards to higher education will clearly become "Do predominantly white colleges and universities want us (Black Students) there and if the answer is yes the question is why?" Do they want us there so that they can provide us with a great education or are we there to meet their federal quota numbers? If we are there for the later, we will never be treated equally. The same is true for HBCUs that aggressively recruit Hispanic students.

If African-American students are not treated fairly at PWIs, they are always welcome to come back home to the institutions that have produced the most African-American graduates since African Americans have been attending Institutions of Higher Education.

Statistical Data on HBCUs that we cannot argue with

According to the National Center on Educational Statistics (NCES) Historically Black Colleges and Universities (HBCUs) are institutions that were established prior to 1964 and have the principal mission of educating Black Americans. As of May 2014 there were 106 official HBCUs designated by the White House Initiative on HBCUs. These institutions were founded and developed in an environment of legal segregation and, by providing access to higher education, contributed substantially to the progress Blacks have made in improving their status. Today, there are 100 HBCUs located in 19 states, the District of Columbia, and the U.S. Virgin Islands. Of the 100 HBCUs, 51 are public institutions and 49 are private, not-for-profit institutions. The number of students enrolled at HBCUs rose by 45 percent between 1976 and 2011, from 223,000 to 324,000. In comparison, total postsecondary enrollment increased by 91 percent, from 11 million to nearly 21 million, during that period.

Although HBCUs were originally founded to educate Black students, they have historically enrolled students other than Black Americans. This diversity has increased over time. In 2011, non-Black students made up 19 percent of enrollment at HBCUs, compared with 15 percent in 1976. Enrollment at HBCUs in 2011 was 61 percent female, up from 53 percent in 1976. In 2011, some 87 percent of HBCU students attended a 4-year institution, while 13 percent attended a 2-year institution. A higher percentage of HBCU students attended public institutions than private, not-for-profit institutions (76 vs. 24 percent). Among Black students, the percentage enrolled at HBCUs has fallen over time, from 18 percent in 1976 to 9 percent in 2011.

In 2010–11, most of the 46,000 degrees conferred by HBCUs were bachelor's degrees (71 percent) and master's degrees (16 percent). Blacks earned 85 percent of the 33,000 bachelor's degrees conferred by HBCUs in that year. At the master's level in 2010–11, Black HBCU students earned 73 percent of the degrees conferred at these institutions. In addition, at both levels, a majority of these degrees were awarded to Black females. Over time, the shares of bachelor's and master's degrees awarded to Blacks by HBCUs have decreased. For example, HBCUs awarded 35 percent of the bachelor's degrees Blacks earned in 1976–77, compared with 16 percent in 2010–11. Additionally, the percentage of Black doctor's degree recipients who received their degrees from HBCUs was one percentage point lower in 2010–11 (13 percent) than in 1976–77 (14 percent).

The total revenue for HBCUs in 2010–11 was $8.5 billion, with $1.7 billion from student tuition and fees. Total expenditures in that year reached $7.7 billion, of which $2.1 billion was spent on instruction.

References

Allen, W. R. (1992). The color of success: African American college student outcomes at predominately White and Historically Black colleges and universities. Harvard Educational Review, 62, p. 26–44.

Allen, W. R., Epps, E., & Haniff, N. Z. (Eds.). (1991). College in black and white: African American students in predominately White and in historically Black public universities. Albany, NY: State University of New York Press.

Altbach, P. (1991). The Racial crisis in American higher education. Albany: State University of New York Press.

Anderson, J. (1988). The education of Blacks in the South, 1860-1935. Chapel Hill: University of North Carolina Press.

Anderson, J.D. (1980). Philanthropic control over private black higher education, In (Ed). Robert Arnove's "In philanthropy and cultural imperialism: The foundations at home and abroad. Boston, MA: Hall & Co.

Baker, J. (2014, September 23). Adjustment of Calculation of Official Three Year Cohort Default Rates for Institutions Subject to Potential Loss of Eligibility. *Information for Financial Aid Professional- Department of education.* (Electronic announcement) retrieved from http://www.ifap.ed.gov/eannouncements/092314AdjustmentofCalculationofOfc3YrCDRforInstit utSubtoPotentialLossofElig.html

Barthelemy, S. J. (1984).*The role of Black Colleges in Nurturing Leadership: Black Colleges and Universities Challenges for the Future*, ed. Antoine Garibaldi New York: Praeger.

Basken, P. & Fuller, A. (2010, April 4). Minority Serving Colleges Do Well in Student Loan Change They Fought. *Chronicle of Higher Education*, 56(30), A1-A25.

Baylor, R. E. (2010). Loss of accreditation at historically Black colleges and universities. New Directions for Higher Education, 2010: 29–38. doi: 10.1002/he.398

Bennett, L. (1988). *Before the Mayflower: A History of Black America*, 6th Ed. New York: Penguin Books (original work published 1961).

Bohr, L, E.T. Pascarella, A. Nora, & P.T. Terenzini (1995). Do black students learn more at historically black colleges or predominately white colleges? *Journal of College Student Development*, 36(1), 75-85.

Brown vs. the Board of Education of Topeka, 347 U.S. 483 (1954)

Burke, L.V. (2013). 125 Year Old HBCU St. Paul's College to Close June 30. Retrieved from http://www.crewof42.com/news/125-year-old-hbcu-st-pauls-college-to-close-june-30/ on April 4, 2015.

Cameron, K. S. (1989). Organizational adaptation and higher education. In M. W. Peterson (Ed.), Organization and governance in higher education (pp. 284–299). Needham Heights, MA: Ginn Press. Constantine, J. M. (1994). Measuring the effect of attending historically Black colleges and universities on future labor market wages on Black students. Paper presented at the Institute for Labor Market Policies, Cornell University, Ithaca, NY.

Carey, K. (2013). The Federal Parent Rip Off Loan. *Chronicle of Higher Education*, 59(38), A60.

Charleston, D. (2014). The United States vs. Waller Co., then me. Prairie View, TX: Charleston Publishing.

Chelsey, R. (2013). Black college's failure should motivate others. *The Virginia Pilot*. Retrieved 10/31/2014.

Creswell, J (2007). Qualitative inquiry & research design: Choosing among five approaches (2nd ed.). Thousand Oaks: Sage Publications.

Cutlip, S.M. (1965). Fundraising in the United States: It's role in American philanthropy. New Brunswick, NJ: Rutgers University Press.

Daufin, E.K., (2001). Minority Faculty Job Experience, Expectations and Job Satisfaction. *Journal & Mass Communication Education*, 18-30.

Davis, J.E. (1994). College in black and white: Campus achievement and academic achievement of African American males. *Journal of Negro Education* 63*(4)*, 620-633.

Devarics, C. (1998). Loan Default Issue Triggers Concern. *Black Issues in Higher Education*, 5(15), 8.

Department of Education, Federal Student Aid Portfolio Performance Division, (2014) Fact Sheet Historical Black Colleges, 12-1 FY 2011 3-Year Cohort Default Rates September. http://www2.ed.gov/offices/OSFAP/defaultmanagement/dmd002.html

Department of Education. Understanding Default: Don't Ignore Your Student Loan Payments or You'll Risking Going Into Default. https://studentaid.ed.gov/repay-loans/default

Department of Education White House Initiative on Historically Black College and Universities.2014. US Department of Education Announces Final Rule to Strengthen Federal Direct PLUS Loan Program.

Drewry, H., & Doermann, H. (2001). Stand and prosper private Black colleges and their students. Princeton, N.J.: Princeton University Press.

Drummond, T. (2001). Black schools go white. Time Almanac 2001, 349.

Evans, A. L., Evans, V., Evans, A. M. (2002). Historically Black Colleges and Universities (HBCUS). Education, 123, 3–16.

Ellison, R. (1952). The invisible man. NewYork, NY: Random House. (p.142).

Fester, R., Gasman, M., & Nguyen, T. (2012). We Know Very Little: Accreditation and Historically Black Colleges and Universities. *Journal of Black Studies*, *43*(7), 806-819. doi:10.1177/0021934712453467

Field, K. (2013). Historically Black Colleges Prepare to Sue over PLUS loan changes. *Chronicle* of Higher Education, 6 (1), 12.

Fields, C. D. (2001, June 21). Parting words. Black Issues in Higher Education, 18, 39–41.

Fleming, J. (1984). Blacks in college. San Francisco, CA:

Foster, G. (1996). Are Black colleges needed? An at risk/prescriptive guide. Kearney, NE: Morris Pub.

Gabbidon, S.L., Greene, H.T., & Wilder, K., (2002). Still Excluded? An Update on The Status of African American scholars in The Discipline of Criminology and Criminal Justice. *Journal of Research in Crime and Delinquency*, 41(4), 384-406.

Gardner, J. W. (1990). On leadership. New York, NY: The Free Press.

Gasman, M. (2012). Vacancies in the black college presidency: What's going on? *Chronicle of Higher Education*. Retrieved 10/31/2014.

Gasman, M. (2007). Envisioning black colleges: A history of the United Negro College Fund. Baltimore, MD: John Hopkins University Press.

Gasman, M. & S. Anderson-Thompkins (2003). Fundraising from black college alumni: Successful strategies for supporting alumni. Washington, DC: CASE Books.

Gasman, M & N. Bowman, III. (2011). A to fundraising at Historically Black Colleges and Universities: An all campus approach. New York, NY: Routledge.

Gasman, M. (2009). Historically Black Colleges and Universities in a Time of Economic Crisis. *Academe*, *95*(6), 26-28.

Gasman, M. & Collins, H. (2014). The Historically Black College and University Community And the Obama Administration: A Lesson in Communication, Change: *The Magazine of Higher Learning*, 46:5, 39-43, DOI:10.1080/00091383.2014.941770

Gasman, M., (2012). Historically Black Colleges and Universities Must Embrace Diversity. *The Chronicle of Higher Education.* Retrieved on 2/10/2015 fromhttp://chronicle.com/blogs

Gasman, M., Baez, B., Drezner, N.D., Sedgwick, K.V., & Tudcio, C., (2007). *Historical Black Colleges and Universities: Recent Trends 2007.*

Graduate Employees and Students Organization (Yale University). (2005). The (un)changing face of the Ivy League. New Haven, Conn.: Graduate Employees and Students Organization, Yale University.

Griffith, J. (1996). Historically Black Colleges and Universities: 1976 to 1994. Retrieved April 7, 2015, from http://nces.ed.gov/pubs/96902.pdf

Godfrey, F. E. (1999, August 5). Diversity—at what price? University Faculty Voice, 3. Hearing before the Subcommittee on Postsecondary Education of the Committee on Education and Labor. (1988). The unique role and mission of historically Black colleges and universities. (Serial No. 100-98). Washington, DC: U.S. Government Printing Office.

Healy, P., (1996). Black College Struggles with Court Order to Recruit Whites. *The Chronicle of Higher Education Faculty.* Retrieved on 2/10/2015 from http://chronicle.com/article/Black-College-Struggles-With/97063/

Heard, C., & Bing, R., (1993). African American Faculty and Students on Predominantly White University Campuses. *Journal of Criminal Justice Education*, 4:1-13.

Henderson, J. (2001). HBCUs will still have a role to play in the 21st century. Black Issues in Higher Education, 17, 128.

Henderson, T. (2001) Graduation rates at NCAA division II HBCUs jump. University Faculty Voice, 5. February 10–11. Historically Black College and University Megasite. Retrieved August 16, 2003 from http://hbcu-central.com.

Holsendolph, E. (1971). Black colleges are worth saving. *Fortune, 84(4)*, 104-107.

Integrated Postsecondary Education Data System (2010-2014). Washington D.C.

Jacobson, J., (2003). Professors Are Finding Better Pay and Freedom at Community Colleges. *The Chronicle of Higher Education Faculty.* Retrieved on 2/10/2015 from http://chronicle.com/article/Professors-Are-Finding-Better/18498/

Jencks, C.& D. Reisman (1967). The American Negro College. *Harvard Educational Review* 39(2).

Jewell, J.O., (2002). To Set An Example The Tradition of Diversity at Historically Black Colleges and Universities. *Urban Education*, 37(1), 7-21.

John, W.C. (1920). Agricultural and Mechanical Colleges, 1917-1918. Washington, DC: U.S. Government Printing Office.

Jones, B. A. (1974). The tradition of sociology teaching in Black colleges: The unheralded profession. In C. V. Willie, M. K. Grady, R. O. Hope, (Eds), African-Americans and the doctoral experience (pp. 8–18). New York, NY: Teachers College Press.

Jones, S. R. (1984). Adapting governance, leadership styles, and management to a changing environment. In A. Garibaldi (Ed.), Black colleges and universities (pp. 268–286). New York, NY: Praeger Publications. National Center for Education Statistics. (1996). Historically Black colleges and universities, 1976–94. (NCES 96-902). Washington, DC: U.S. Government Printing Office.

Jones, T.J. (1969). Negro education: A study of private and public higher education schools for colored people in the United States. New York, NY: Arno Press.

Jossey-Bass. Foster, L. H. (1987). The hazards in Black higher education: Institutional management. Journal of Negro Education, 56, 137–144.

Kelderman, E. (2010). White House Pledges Continuing Federal Support for Historically Black Colleges. *The Chronicle of Higher Education Faculty*. Retrieved on 2/10/2015 from http://chronicle.com/article/White-House-Reaches-Out-to/124389/

Kim, M.M. (2002). Historically Black vs. White institutions: Academic development among Black students. *The Review of Higher Education*, 25, 385-407.

Lee, J.M. and Keys, S.W. (2013). *Impact of Parent PLUS Loan Changes on Historically Black Colleges and Universities.* (APLU Office of Access and Success publication no. 3000-7S1). Washington, DC: Association of Public and Land-grant Universities.

Lee, J.M. and Keys, S.W. (2013). *Repositioning HBCUs for the Future: Access, Success, Research & Innovation.* (APLU Office of Access and Success Discussion Paper 2013-01). Washington, DC: Association of Public and Land-grant Universities.

McPherson, J.M., (1975). The abolitionist legacy: From reconstruction to the NAACP. Princeton, NJ: Princeton University Press.

Mahan, S.M. (2011, May 12) Federal Pell Grant Program of the Higher Education Act: Recent Changes, and Current Legislative Issues. *Congressional Research Service.*

Malveaux, J. (2013, September 11). Obama Metrics Would Hurt Historically Black Colleges. *USA Today*, P.6A

Maxwell, B. (2013, June 18) For Black Colleges, A Key Role. *Tampa Bay Times*. P. 3.

Millette, R. (2005). Leadership and Shared Governance at Historically Black Colleges and Universities: Observations and Recommendations. Retrieved April 7, 2015, from http://www.lincoln.edu/history/journal/millette1.htm

Missouri ex rel. Gaines v. Canada, 305 U.S. 337 (1938)

Morris, C. (2014) HBCUs on Edge. *Diverse Issues in Education* 31(19), 12-13.

Mullins, D. (2013). H*istorically black colleges in financial fight for their future: Institutions assert their relevance amid financial concerns, falling enrollment.* Retrieved from http://america.aljazeera.com/articles/2013/10/22/historically-blackcollegesfightfortheirfuture.html on October 20, 2014.

Myrdal, G. (1944). An American dilemma. New York, NY: David McKay (pg. 304).

National Center of Education Statistics, (2012). HBCU Financial Aid. *IPEDS*. 2009-2012.

Nelson, L. A. (2012, October 12). Cracking Down on PLUS Loans *Inside Higher Education*. Retrieved from https://www.insidehighered.com/news/2012/10/12/standards-tightening-federal-plus-loans

O'Brien, K.M. (2012) African American male student athletes: Identity and academic performance. Dissertation.

Office of the Federal Register, (2014, August 8). William D. Ford Direct Loan Program: Notice of proposed rulemaking press release. Press Media Solutions.

Painter, N.I., (2000). Black Studies, Black Professors, and the Struggles of Perception. *The Chronicle of Higher Education Faculty*. Retrieved on 2/10/2015 from http://chronicle.com/article/Black-Studies-Black/9522/

Penn, E.B. & Gabbidon, S. L. (2007). Criminal Justice Education at Historically Black Colleges and Universities: Three Decades of Progress. Journal of Criminal Justice Education, vol. 18, no. 1 (March 2007), 137-162.

Plata, M. (1996). Retaining ethnic minority faculty at institutions of higher education. *Journal of Instructional Psychology*, 23(3), 221-227.

Plessy vs. Ferguson, 163 U.S. 537 (1896)

Provansik, S., & Shafer, L.L., (2004). *Historically Black Colleges and Universities*, 1976 to 2001 (NCES 2004-062). U.S. Department of Education, National Center for Educational Statistics. Washington, DC: Government Printing Office.

Richards, D.A.R. (2014.).Lower Costs, Higher Returns: UNCF HBCUs in a High-Priced College Environment. *Washington, DC: Fredrick D. Patterson Research Institute, UNFC.* Retrieved from http://www.uncf.org/fdpri/Portals/0/fdpri.Lower-CostsHigher-Returns.pdf

Rivard, R. (2014, June 24). Public HBCU'S facing Tests on Many Fronts, Fight for Survival. *Inside Higher Education.* Retrieved from *https://www.insidehighered.com/news/2014/06/24/*.

Rooks, C.S. (1967, April 14). Letter to *Time* magazine.

Samuels, A. L. (2004) Is Separate Unequal? Black Colleges and the Challenges to Desegregation (Kansas: University Press of Kansas.

Stratford, M. & Paul Fain. (September, 2014 25). Default Rates Dip Slightly. *Inside Higher Education.* Retrieved from https://www.insidehighered.com/news/2014/09/25/default-rate-federal-loans-ticks-down-slightly-21-colleges-face-sanctions-high-rates

Stratford, M. (April, 2014 3). Default Data on Parent PLUS Loans. *Inside Higher Education.* Retrieved from https://www.insidehighered.com/news/2014/04/03/education-department-releases-default-data-controversial-parent-plus-loans

Stratford, M. (September, 2014 24). Reprieve on Defaults. *Inside Higher Education.* Retrieved from https://www.insidehighered.com/news/2014/09/24/education-dept-tweaks-default-rate-calculation-help-colleges-avoid-penalties

The Top Colleges for African Americans. (2000, June 14). Black College Monthly, The Time Almanac 2000. 1999. Borgna Brunner (Ed.). Boston, MA: Family Education Co.

Thompson, D. C. (1986). A Black elite: A profile of graduates of UNCF colleges. Westport, CT: Greenwood. United States Department of the Interior. (n.d.) Historically Black Colleges and Universities. Retrieved May 28, 2002, from http://www.doi.gov/hrm/black.html. Wagener, U., & Samuels, A. L. (2004) Is Separate Unequal? Black Colleges and the Challenges to Desegregation Kansas: University Press of Kansas.

Sanders v. Ellington, 288 F. Supp. 937 (1968)

Schneider, A., (1999). Union College Limits Search for 4 New Faculty Slots to Black and Hispanic Scholars. *The Chronicle of Higher Education Faculty.* Retrieved on 2/10/2015 from http://chronicle.com/article/Union-College-Limits-Search/13082/

Schneider, A., (2000). 5 White Professors Sue a Black College for Race Discrimination. *The Chronicle of Higher Education Faculty.* Retrieved on 2/10/2015 from http://chronicle.com/article/5-White-Professors-Sue-a-Black/32433

Sowell, T. (1972). Black education: Myths and tragedies. New York, NY: McKay.

Sipuel v. Board of Regents of University of Oklahoma, 332 U.S. 631 (1948)

Sowell, T.W. (1973). Black education: Myths and tragedies. New York, NY: David Mckay

Stratford, M. & Paul Fain. (September, 2014 25). Default Rates Dip Slightly. *Inside Higher Education.* Retrieved from https://www.insidehighered.com/news/2014/09/25/default-rate-federal-loans-ticks-down-slightly-21-colleges-face-sanctions-high-rates

Stratford, M. (April, 2014 3). Default Data on Parent PLUS Loans. *Inside Higher Education.* Retrieved from https://www.insidehighered.com/news/2014/04/03/education-department-releases-default-data-controversial-parent-plus-loans

Stratford, M. (September, 2014 24). Reprieve on Defaults. *Inside Higher Education.* Retrieved from https://www.insidehighered.com/news/2014/09/24/education-dept-tweaks-default-rate-calculation-help-colleges-avoid-penalties

Sum. P., Light., & R. King. (2004). "Race, Reform, and Desegregation in Mississippi Higher Educaiton: Historically Black Institutions after United States v. Forcide" *Law and Social Inquiry* 29: 403-436.

Sweatt v. Painter, 339 U.S. 629 (1950)

Trent, W.J., Jr. (1981) Interview by Marcia Goodson. United Negro College Fund Oral History Collection.

Thompson, D.C. (1973). Private colleges at the crossroads. Westport, CT: Praeger.

UNF Fredrick D. Patterson Research Institute. (2014). The Parent PLUS Loan Crisis: An Urgent Crisis Facing Students at the Nation's HBCUs. UNCF.org Washington, DC.

U.S. Department of Education, White House Initiative on Historically Black Colleges and Universities, *2011 Annual Report the President on the Results of the Participation of Historically Black Colleges and Universities in Federal Programs*, Washington, D.C., 2014.

United States Department of Education (1991). *Historically Black Colleges and Universities and Higher Education Desegregation.* Office of Civil Rights. Washington. D.C.

United States Department of Education (2005). *Historically Black Colleges and Universities and Higher Education Desegregation.* Office of Civil Rights. Washington. D.C.

US News. (2015). *HBCU lifestyle: hbcu rankings-2015-top25.* Retrieved from http:hbculifestyle.com

US News. (2015). *HBCUs with high graduation rates.* Retrieved from http://www.usnews.com/education/slideshows.

U.S. v. Fordice, 505 U.S. 717 (1992)

Wenglinsky, H. H. (1996). The educational justification of historically Black colleges and university: A policy response to the U.S. Supreme Court. Educational Evaluation and Policy Analysis, 18, 91–103. Willie, C. V., Grady, M. K., Hope, R. O. (1991). African-Americans and he doctoral experience. New York, NY: Teachers College P

Wilkerson, R. (2005). Aiding Students Buying Students: Financial Aid in America. New York: *Vanderbilt Press.*

Williams, J. & Ashley, D. (2004). I'll find a Way or Make One: A Tribute to Historically Black Colleges and Universities. New York: Harper Collins Publishers.

Wilson, R (1995). Finding and Keeping Black Professors, Old Dominion University faces challenges in recruiting and retaining minority faculty members. *The Chronicle of Higher Education Faculty.* Retrieved on 2/10/2015 from http://chronicle.com/article/FindingKeeping-Black/83724/

Wilson, R., (2000). What Does It Mean When a College Hires 5 Black Scholars? *The Chronicle of Higher Education Faculty.* Retrieved on 2/10/2015 from http://chronicle.com/article/What-Does-It-Mean-When-a/14065/

Made in the USA
Columbia, SC
23 September 2020